RESEARCH ON EMBRYOS:

POLITICS, THEOLOGY AND LAW

RESEARCH ON EMBRYOS:

POLITICS, THEOLOGY AND LAW

Paul A. B. Clarke

Andrew Linzey

With a Foreword by The Very Revd. Dr. John Moses

LESTER CROOK ACADEMIC

Publishing

Lester Crook Academic Publishing,
London House,
271-273 King Street,
Hammersmith,
London W6 9LZ

Copyright 1988 Paul A. B. Clarke and Andrew Linzey.

All rights reserved; no part of this publication may be reproduced, stored in a retrieval system, or transmitted in any form or by any means, electronic, mechanical, photocopying, recording, or otherwise, without prior written permission of the publishers.

ISBN 1 870915 03 8

CONTENTS

About the Authors

Acknowledgements

Foreword
by The Very Revd. Dr. John Moses,
Provost of Chelmsford

1. **Introduction** 11

2. **Politics and Law** 15

Genes and all that 17
Persons 20
The moral community 23
Identity and individuation 29
The initial argument restated 32

3. **Theology and Ethics** 37

The least among us 37
The moral priority of the weak 38
The moral status of the embryo 41
Embryos as potential humans 41
Unsoulled humans 42
Embryos as non-persons 42
Drawing the line 43

Arguments against (i) Individualist ethics 45
(ii) The need to compromise 47
(iii) Uacceptable consequences 48
(iv) Taking power for God 51
The realities of power 54
Dominion or despotism 55
Jesus and powerlessness 56
Moral imagination 58
Otiose arguments 59
Conclusion 60

4. **Submission: The Limits to Embryonic Research** 63

Introduction 63
The creation of embryos 67
Experimentation 72
The moral status of the embryo 80
Recommendations 85

5. **Conclusion** 91

Notes 97

Bibliography 103

ABOUT THE AUTHORS

Paul A. B. Clarke is lecturer in political philosophy in the Department of Government, University of Essex and Fellow of The Centre for the Study of Theology in the University of Essex. His recent publications include, *The Autonomy of Politics*, Avebury 1988, and *AIDS: Medicine, Politics and Society,* Lester Crook Academic, 1988. *The Legal, Political and Moral Status of the Embryo* is due to be published by Lester Crook Academic in late 1988.

Andrew Linzey is Chaplain and Director of Studies, Centre for the Study of Theology in the University of Essex. He has written extensively on aspects of christian ethics and is author of five books, the latest of which is *Christianity and the Rights of Animals*, published in 1987 by SPCK. He is author, with Francoise Hampson, of *Theology, Law and the Use of Armed Force* forthcoming from Lester Crook Academic.

ACKNOWLEDGEMENTS

Our special thanks go to Peter Wexler of the University of Essex for his erudite comments on earlier drafts of Chapter Two of this book. His advice was invaluable, but of course responsibility for the work is entirely our own.

We would like to thank the Centre for the Study of Theology at the University of Essex, for its support and encouragement of our project, Dr. John Moses, Provost of Chelmsford and Chairman of the Council of the Centre for his kind foreword to the book, and not least of all to Dr. Lester Crook for his efficient publishing assistance.

Louis MacNeice's poem, 'Prayer before Birth', reprinted by permission of Faber and Faber Ltd. from *The Collected Poems of Louis MacNeice*.

P.A.B.C.

A.L.

FOREWORD

The Centre for the Study of Theology in the University of Essex is concerned to bring together, from different disciplines, scholars who wish to examine the implications of Christian theology for the complex issues which confront our society to-day.

I welcome the fact that the Centre's first publication is addressing the question of embryonic research. There are few matters that raise more sharply our understanding of the concept of a person, the responsibilities of a compassionate and moral society, the insights of the Christian revelation for contemporary issues, and the consequences that can follow the institutionalisation through legislation of experimental practice.

Dr. Paul Clarke and Dr. Andrew Linzey have explored these issues with great thoroughness and sensitivity. They have challenged the inevitability of embryonic research. They have examined the political, legal, ethical and theological considerations which must inform our decisions. They have attempted to identify the purposes of God in His self-revelation in Jesus Christ. They have raised questions concerning the function of legislation and the realities of power that are contained within this subject. They have pleaded for greater imagination in our thinking about unborn human life if we are to have a sense of solidarity with, and respect for, our human origins.

This work is being published so that the arguments and submissions contained within it might be allowed to contribute to public debate and decision-making. Many will welcome the unambiguous statement concerning the 'marker event' at which human life can properly be said to begin. Many will be grateful for the distinction that is made between therapeutic *intervention* and therapeutic *research*. All Christian people will endorse the strong emphasis that the mystery of God's love gives to every human being - and to all who have the potential to become human beings - an irreducible value.

JOHN MOSES
Chairman of the Council of the
Centre for The Study of Theology

February 1988

1

INTRODUCTION

In 1982 the Committee of Inquiry into Human Fertilisation and Embryology was established. Its terms of reference were:

> To consider recent and potential developments in medicine and science related to human fertilisation and embryology; to consider what policies and safeguards should be applied, including consideration of the social, ethical and legal implications of these developments and to make recommendations.[1]

The terms of reference made it quite clear that the Government regarded the issues raised by I.V.F. (In Vitro Fertilisation) techniques, and the corollary of embryonic research, as raising not only medical questions but also social and ethical questions. Much of the evidence to the Committee reflected those concerns and in its final report, published in 1984, many of the arguments which had lead to the recommendations were couched in ethical and philosophical terms. Clearly the issues raised by I.V.F. techniques went far beyond the purely medical, impinging into areas of philosophy, ethics, theology, sociology and even politics. As a moral issue it seems that only the abortion debate has raised the same kind of public concern as the question of embryonic research.

It is embryonic research rather than I.V.F. treatment as such that has raised moral concerns. By itself I.V.F. treatment is seen by many as largely uncontentious. If I.V.F. were merely one means of dealing with infertility and was otherwise morally cost free it is doubtful that it would have generated enough interest to justify a full committee of inquiry.

However, I.V.F. is not morally cost free. Minimally it requires the production of embryos in vitro which may not be implanted, or maximally it requires the implantation of an excessive number of embryos which, should they take, may lead to the necessity of what is often referred to as 'selective termination'. At the point of 'selective termination', the production of children to an otherwise infertile couple actually requires the deliberate decision to abort some apparently normal foetuses. Such practices are, admittedly, rare. Following the publication of the Warnock Committee's report, a Voluntary Licensing Authority (V.L.A.) was established with the aim of regulating I.V.F. techniques and embryonic research in line with those recommendations. Massive multiple implantation was discouraged as was embryonic research outside of the Warnock guidelines. However, at least one clinic systematically ignored those guidelines and it was clear the the V.L.A. was powerless to prevent the moral dilemma of sacrificing some potential human lives in order to aid the possible production of other human lives. There was, and could be, no guarantee that the V.L.A. guidelines would not be broken in the area of embryonic research.

Embryonic research arose primarily as a result of I.V.F. techniques. In the nature of those techniques it may well be, and often is, the case that so called 'spare embryos'; that is embryos which have been fertilised but which have not, and probably will not be implanted, become available for both observation and experimentation. Those who favour such research argued that, as the destruction of such embryos was almost certainly inevitable, their use as objects of research may well benefit society as a whole. No harm could result from such research but the potential benefit could be enormous. Those objecting to such research argued that the embryo had some moral status and was entitled to respect by virtue of that moral status. There are, of course, a number of variants on these themes - some deployed with considerable skill and subtlety and some expressed with considerable crudity. What was clear, was that whatever view one might take, some kind of Parliamentary decision with respect to I.V.F. and to embryonic research was required before events overtook the uneasy moral consensus that the V.L.A. had established, but which was increasingly shown to be breaking down.

The Government's next step was to issue a consultation document, Cm 46 on Human Infertility Services and Embryo Research, in which it outlined the options that it thought appropriate to include in a legislative programme. That document made it clear that while there would be no attempt to limit I.V.F. treatment as such, it would be appropriate to control clinics offering I.V.F. treatment. The provisions of the Surrogacy Arrangements Act 1985 would be extended and Members of Parliament would be given a free vote on whether or not embryonic research up to a period of fourteen days should be allowed. In responding to Cm 46 [2], we made it clear that the wording in the two optional clauses that were to be offered to Members of Parliament was such that it was far from clear that the two optional clauses were mutually exclusive.

In a further document, Cm 259 *Human Fertilisation and Embryology: A Framework for Legislation,*[3] the Government's legislative intentions, in general terms, have been made clearer and the wording of the optional clauses on embryonic research has been altered broadly in line with our suggestions. [4] However, the wording is still not as precise as we would wish and the concerns that we expressed in our response to Cm 46: namely that Parliamentary responses might be thwarted by a failure of precise wording of the appropriate optional clauses, still holds.

It is the Government's intention that Cm 259 be debated in principle in Parliament prior to bringing forward a Bill for consideration by Parliament. Some elements of that Bill are fixed and not open to further consultation and will not be the subject of a free vote. Only the issue of embryonic research is genuinely open.

In what follows we hope to expand and contribute to the present debate by outlining political, theological and philosophical arguments which support the case that we wish to maintain. While those arguments have different starting points, they converge to produce what we hope is a coherent, interdisciplinary underpinning for the case that we made to the Government in a submission in mid 1987. We also hope that these arguments will be timely in that they will both inform and expand the present legislative debate, while being of sufficient timelessness to transcend the immediacy of that present debate.

2

POLITICS AND LAW

The arguments either in favour of, or against, embryonic research can be quite complex. Cm 46 summarised the arguments in favour of such research in the claim that:

> Those who support embryo research would not generally accept the position that the embryo should, from the point of conception, be regarded as having the same full human status as a child. Thus they would say that moral arguments based on that premise are misplaced. They would also say that research which could help to alleviate human suffering and handicap has its own moral imperative.[5]

Arguments against research are summarised in the claim that:

> Those who are opposed to any research involving human embryos argue that embryos, from the point of conception, have the same status as that of a child or an adult. It would thus be improper to conduct research on them which would lead to their eventual destruction. The embryo should be seen as fully human because of its potential for human life, the right to life being the most fundamental of all human rights. It is therefore held that research which leads to the destruction of an embryo is tantamount to murder as the embryo does not have the opportunity to fulfil its potential.[6]

It is clear that both summaries contain some powerful appeals, though it is less than clear whether either can constitute a full and coherent philosophical argument with satisfactory empirical backing. Generally legislatures have backed away from endowing the conceptus with the right to life. To our knowledge the only serious exception has been the American Convention on Human Rights 1969, inaugurated on 3rd September 1979, article 4.1 of which states that:

> Every person has the right to have his life respected. This right shall be protected by law, and in general, from the moment of conception...[7]

It may well be that a good case can be made out for the claims embodied in article 4.1, but that is not our case, and not part of our argument and to that extent at least any claim made in para. 52 of Cm 46 which rests on such a claim is not presently part of our case. Our argument is somewhat different composing of two principal elements. First, that the claims of Cm 46 are incoherent and lead to fundamental contradictions, and second, that the model that we would wish to adopt with regard to the embryo is based less on the notion of rights and more on the notion of duties: in this case the notion of duties is expressed best by the stewardship or guardianship model. We believe it is this model that actually underlies the bulk of the arguments in Cm 259 relating to surrogacy and that there is a disjunction between the proposed (and non optional) proposals relating to surrogacy arrangements in Cm 259 and the proposals relating to embryonic research. In other words, the proposals of Cm 259 adopt one set of criteria with respect to surrogacy arrangements: arrangements which rest on the stewardship model, and adopt another model: namely absolute property arrangements with respect to the clause permitting embryonic research. We find this difference of standards applied to an entity of the same moral status (however that might be understood and articulated, extremely disturbing). The balance of this part of our argument will be concerned with uncovering some of the difficulties in the case presented by the DHSS in Cm 259.

Genes and All That

It goes almost without saying that there are a welter of philosophical and sociological arguments which see life as either not genetically based, or see genetic claims about the basis of life as important only insofar as such claims represent the manifestation of certain social forces within society. It is not our concern here to deal with such arguments. Powerful though such argument may seem to some, our concern is with the practical ethics of genetic research as we find it. To that extent we take certain practical claims as axiomatic. We take it that the genetic manipulation of the origins of life has some practical and moral import. In turn this claim rests on a prior understanding that:

a) genetic structures are (in some way) an indispensable basis of human life,

and

b) the basis of human life has some moral claim upon us.

Proposition a) is taken here merely as a matter of practical reason: it is outside our present remit to understand it in any other way. Proposition b) could be taken in the strong sense evidenced in, for example, the American Convention in which case the ascription of rights to the conceptus would follow, or it could be taken in a weak sense: namely that human life has some worth hence the basis of that life has some worth. In general if we accept that human life has some hold upon us then the weak sense also has some hold on us. The simplest way to demonstrate this is to imagine a case where we took it as a principle that the basis of human life had no hold on us. The corollary of such a view would be that we would be compelled to adopt a principle that the future of the human race, and any duties that we might have to the existence or being of that future, had no claim upon us. Such a view is not logically inconsistent but it is not one that could be reasonably, or even logically, accepted by either side in this particular debate. The claim that embryonic research could help alleviate suffering in the future already implies a sense of duty to the future. Hence, we must assume that the proponents of embryonic research feel some duty to the future and to future generations. The weak view, as expressed above, that the basis of human life has some worth is, therefore, a view that is logically implied in views for and against embryonic research. It is this weak, and by implication commonly held view, that provides our basic premise.

It should be noted, if only in passing at this point, that holding,

b) the basis of human life has some moral claim upon us,

does not preclude us from holding,

b' the basis of any form of life has some moral claim upon us.

Holding b) does not, therefore, preclude us from holding wider claims about different forms of life or different species of life. Nor does it, and this might seem surprising in the context of our case, preclude us from denying that the basis of human life is itself a person (as some might claim and which claim seems to be implied in the American Convention). Hence b) is quite compatible with the claim that,

c) the genetic basis of human life is not a person,

and, if this is the case, then holding b) does not commit us to the view that the conceptus or zygote is a person, and it does not commit us to the view that the destruction of embryos is equivalent to homicide. At this point the common ground which we found between the views which Cm 46 and Cm 259 represented as opposing views disappears and the differences become clear. The destruction of a human person is presumably classed as homicide and that is the basis of part of the argument of para. 52 of Cm 46.

However, acceptance of this divergence from common ground does not commit us to a view that embryonic research is to be sanctioned. On the contrary, our premises can be expanded to show the difficulties of para. 51 of Cm 46, and the fact that some common ground is shared between us and the advocates of Cm 46, enhances our case. Briefly our argument runs as follows:

b) the basis of human life has some moral claim upon us;

c) the genetic basis of human life is not itself a person;

d) the destruction of a conceptus or zygote is not tantamount to homicide;

e) nevertheless the destruction of a zygote (or any other action) is not warranted by some mere (putative) or informed claim to benefit.

f) therefore the claim that 'research which could help to alleviate human suffering and handicap has its own moral imperative and justification' (Cm. 46 para. 51, is not self-sufficient).

g) Hence the arguments of S. 51 fail even on their own terms and do not provide a justification for embryonic research.

At first sight this might seem a strange case to make. It departs from some of the assumptions of S. 52 of Cm 46 in important respects and even shares some common ground with the views of those advocating embryonic research as outlined in S. 51 of Cm 46. Some of the assumptions in b) to g) follow quite clearly from the minimal argument already presented. Some of the assumptions and arguments do, however, require some expansion. In the following sections we will attempt to explain some of the reasoning behind the propositions outlined in b) to g).

Persons

A great deal of philosophical energy has been expended in attempting to outline what might or might not count as a person. Some confusion arises as a result of the tradition from which the writer develops his or her exposition. To give an example: in one Catholic tradition a distinction is made between persons and things. Hence an embryo being not a thing is automatically a person. It is this kind of reasoning which appears to underlie the summary given in S. 52 of Cm 46 and which leads to the view that 'zygocide' (our term) is equivalent to homicide. This is a view which, as it stands, we cannot accept. It is one thing to say that intentional harm to zygotes is morally and (should be) legally wrong, it is another to say that such harm is morally and (should legally be) equivalent to homicide.

Clearly we feel that the concept of a person does not easily apply to a conceptus; at the very least considerable philosophical and legal development of the concept of a person would be required before we would find that notion easy to accept. The notion of a person is, admittedly, a difficult one and we would accept that its full implications have not been fully worked through and that there is room for further development of the notion. However, as we take it, the notion of a person can be expressed in three different ways: first, as a legal notion and here the American Convention does provide the paradigm case of the right to life being given, generally, from the moment of conception. It is notable that the American Convention expresses that right in terms of the notion of a person rather than in terms of the notion of a human being. We are, therefore, persuaded that the legal definition of a person could be extended to the conceptus. However, the notion of a person is also a metaphysical/moral notion and as such occupies a considerable amount of philosophical literature. Outside of the tradition mentioned above we are not aware of any serious arguments in philosophy which could (yet) treat the conceptus as a person. The notion of a person is also an empirical matter at least in the sense that once the criteria of a person are determined, what is or is not a person is a matter for empirical, even scientific, determination.

What is important about our conception of a person is that we claim no legal, philosophical or empirical exclusivity for that concept. The legal, philosophical and empirical criteria are not mutually exclusive, they serve rather as a series of checks and balances so that a 'person' might be a term having a legal expression of some moral and metaphysical criteria which are empirically determined. This kind of understanding of a 'person' could be met by several contemporary philosophical accounts of what it is to be a person. One practical account of what it is to be a human being was given by Peter Singer in evidence to the Australian Senate Select Committee on *Human Embryo Experimentation in Australia*:

> A human being is a being possessing, at least at a minimal level, the capacities distinctive of our species, which include consciousness, the ability to relate to others, perhaps even rationality and self consciousness.[8]

This account cannot be regarded as a sufficient definition of a person. It contains, we observe, some important qualifications: particularly that relating to capacity. It is not the actual presence of certain qualities which makes a being count as a human being. If that were the case then a human being asleep would not be a human being at all for the quality of sentience or consciousness would be lacking. However, for our purposes, while the question of what does or does not count as a human being might be counted as interesting, it is less directly relevant to our needs than what counts (or does not count) as a person. This is not to say that some knowledge is not gained from Singer's remarks. The qualification made with respect to the capacities of human beings will apply also to persons.

Some confusion frequently arises between the concepts of a human being, a person, and a human person. Clearly our understanding of persons is derived from our practical and theoretical understanding of human persons, but there is no self-evident requirement that the notion of a person be limited to *human* persons. Hence we might regard the terms, human being, and, person, as class terms which may or may not overlap in certain ways. The term, human being, we suggest, is more a biological term, than the notion of person. While human beings are persons, and while our practical and empirical knowledge of what counts as a person is derived from our practical and empirical knowledge of human beings - at least in the first instance, it does not necessarily follow that all possible persons are human beings. This is the non-biological attribute view of persons or what David Wiggins calls the 'animal attribute view' of persons.

> This sees person as a concept whose defining marks are to be given in terms of a natural kind determinable, say animal plus what may be called a functional or (as I shall prefer to say) systemic component. Perhaps x is a person if and only if x is an animal falling under an extension of a kind whose typical members perceive, feel, remember, imagine, desire, make projects, move themselves at will, speak, carry out projects, acquire a character as they age, are happy or miserable, are susceptible to concern for members of their own or like species... conceive of themselves as perceiving, feeling, remembering, imagining, desiring, making projects, speaking... have and conceive of themselves as having a past accessible in experience- memory and a future accessible in intention...[9]

Whether one would wish to include all of these non-biological attributes in the concept of a person, or indeed whether one would wish to add more, is a matter of philosophical debate. What does seem clear is that if this general model of personhood is accepted then the notion of a person is not necessarily restricted to human beings. It may be that:

> the extension of person should give hospitality to such creatures as chimpanzees or dolphins... According to this view, a person is any animal that is such by its kind to enjoy fully the psychological attributes enumerated; and whether or not a given animal kind qualifies is left to be a strictly empirical matter.[10]

Our understanding of a person does not then, a-priori exclude a conceptus from being a person. Our view of a person can quite easily encompass legal, metaphysical/moral and empirical domains. Hence whether a conceptus, or a foetus, is a person is a matter to be empirically determined and which, if so determined, can easily find legal expression. As of this moment in time, however, there is no empirical evidence of which we are aware which could lead us to regard the conceptus as a person in the sense enumerated above. On the other hand, we would express the point that being a person is not something that happens at a certain point in time. There is no sudden transition in the normal development of human life between being a human being which is not yet a person and being a human being who is also a person. This leads us to two further observations of import: first, in the development of human life one grows into personhood, and second, that there is no marker point at which it is possible to say when a particular human being or when any human being, in general, will be a person.

It might be objected against this view that the conceptus manifestly fails to meet the empirical criteria of personhood and is not, therefore, yet deserving of the respect which is accorded to that status. Set against this, however, we would maintain that, given the developmental nature of human personhood, the human embryo is deserving of respect by virtue of its orientation towards the development of full personhood. On those grounds alone the embryo is deserving of respect and of care. Indeed, it could be argued that such human beings *in transition* to full personhood deserve in a caring society, *more* protection than others already recognisably 'persons'. For example: Are newly born children 'persons'? The question is at least arguable, and yet few would not commend special care and consideration towards the newly born in our society.

The Moral Community

A being, or individual, might be said to be deserving of respect on several grounds. It may be that there is something intrinsic to that individual which is good in itself and which requires no further justification for respect. It may be that the individual, and here that term is used in its logical sense, is valued by some other: that is to say, it has extrinsic value or it may be, as in the case of an individual who is a person and has the capacity of being, as Wiggins puts it, 'susceptible to concern for their own or like species'. For such a being is capable of being a part of a moral community and both gives and receives respect by virtue of that membership.

Members of a moral community are normally regarded as being moral agents: that is to say, they have the capacity to, and generally do, act towards others in a manner that betokens respect for others as ends in themselves and not as mere means, or as mere resources, for some end or purpose of their own. A moral community is not so limited or restricted, however. Children, particularly young children, are perhaps a paradigm case. Though young children cannot be regarded as having duties they can be regarded as having rights. Those rights accrue to them by virtue of their intrinsic value, by virtue of their value to others and by virtue of their membership of a moral community. Young children meet all three criteria for respect and yet do not have duties towards the community and cannot, therefore, be said to be moral agents; they are moral patients, and being a moral patient should not in itself indicate a lack of value.

At any time a moral agent may lapse into a condition of being a moral patient. For example: sleep, which is a temporary state of unconsciousness, renders a moral agent impotent. But rights, and perhaps even duties, do not end with sleep. In that condition a person still has the capacity to act as an agent and so retains all the respect due to moral agents. In an ideal world we would expect a moral community to be constructed on purely altruistic grounds, but even if this were not possible, it is in one's self interest to help construct, maintain, and retain membership of a moral community. It is egoistically desirable to reduce the condition of naked fear of which Hobbes wrote so graphically: a condition in which even the strongest is prey to the machinations of the weakest.

If membership of a moral community is desirous so, in our world at least, is membership of a legal community; particularly when that legal community is based on moral imperatives. Such membership brings with it guarantees that might otherwise be lacking and add security to life in an otherwise uncertain world. We have written of the developmental notion of a person and have referred to the membership of the moral community of young children who are not themselves moral agents. This leads to the question as to what criteria have to be met before membership of the moral community is regarded as having been satisfied.

The obvious criteria would appear to be birth and in most Western countries at least that is the legal criteria. Indeed in this country the legal criteria, as laid down in the Infant Life Preservation Act of 1929, is 'viability'. That notion, recently interpreted in a test case[11], was said to be the capacity to breathe independently. However, the defined point of viability is continually changing and is presently placed by the World Health Organisation, at twenty weeks after conception. Western criteria in this area have, however, to a large extent been imposed upon other societies, where a period after birth is sometimes stipulated; often the process of naming is taken as crucial. Whatever the exact criteria, it is important to any moral community to lay down some fixed and intrinsic standard after which membership of that community is irrevocable. Embryonic research and its possible effects have merely heightened the search for some kind of marker event beyond which research should not be permitted. The difficulty is finding such a marker event. But whatever the difficulties, the importance of the task cannot be underestimated, as Margaret Somerville said in giving evidence to the Australian Senate Select Committee:

> One good legal reason for choosing such an event is to differentiate and disidentify one group of human cells (embryos) from another group of cells (the rest of us) in order to ensure that precedents set with embryos do not apply to us..... In short we must ensure that our differential treatment of human entities is inherently justified and not just a result of extrinsic labels that we attach for the purpose of legitimating certain conduct.[12]

Clearly such an intrinsic differentiation is important. In the worst case, if no differentiation could be made, then experiments carried out on embryos could with full justification be carried out on any member of the community. Some intrinsic and inherent point of a change of value is required before any form of experimentation on a non-consenting subject can be justified. Yet this was what the Warnock Committee were unable to find. Thus the majority report was forced to conclude that:

> While, as we have seen, the timing of the different stages of development is critical, once the process has begun there is no particular part of the developmental process that is more important than another; all are part of a continuous process, and unless each stage takes place normally, at the correct time, and in the correct sequence, further development will cease. Thus biologically there is no one single identifiable stage in the development of the embryo beyond which the in vitro embryo should not be kept alive. *However we agreed that this was an area in which some precise decision must be taken, in order to allay public anxiety.*[13]

And this is a clear case of extrinsic criteria being used to solve a problem which requires the determination of firm and unequivocal intrinsic criteria. By adopting this particular approach the Warnock Committee admitted that no intrinsic criteria could be found which differentiated the embryo at any stage of its development and yet the Committee still wished to permit some embryonic experimentation. The ultimate justification for the fourteen day period was purely taken with a view to allaying 'public anxiety'.

The effect of being unable to determine any clear intrinsic criteria which would 'differentiate and disidentify one group of human cells (embryos) from another group of cells (the rest of us)' does raise the danger of setting precedents to which Margaret Somerville is quite right to point, but it also has other consequences. First, if we are unable to determine clear criteria by which we should exclude one group of entities from the moral community then it seems that, on the grounds of self interest alone, such entities whether they be moral agents or moral patients should by presumption be included in the moral community. The appeal here is relatively clear: if some group of entities are excluded on extrinsic grounds then it might be the case that any group of entities could be excluded on extrinsic grounds. In terms of self-interest alone that reduces the security of anyone and everyone in the moral community: a community whose boundaries are potentially subject to arbitrary change. In such a case no one is entirely safe and the Hobbesian spectre raises itself. If a more modern parallel is required, the Nazi declassification of some human beings, namely Jews, Gypsies and the like, to the status of 'sub-human' beings should suffice to show the real political possibilities. The avoidance of such political moves can be guaranteed only within a political, legal and moral culture that mitigates against such disidentification. Distinctions between 'us' and 'them' need to be firmly grounded and not left to the political whims of the day.

Second, within the confines of the moral community it is clear that the claim made in para. 51 Cm 46 i.e., 'research which could help to alleviate human suffering and handicap has its own moral imperative and justification' cannot hold without qualification. If that imperative is held without qualification then the underlying philosophical perspective that is revealed is one of unqualified utilitarianism. In classical utilitarianism the only sanction that is required is that the action taken, whatever its personal consequences for the person upon whom the action is taken, must benefit the greater good. In such a stark form almost any form of experimentation might be justified in terms of 'benefit'. But it is also clear that in such stark form the experimentee is being used as a mere means and not as an end in him or herself: some aspect of intrinsic human dignity is being overlooked or avoided. Again the history of certain forms of political regime have demonstrated the reality of such a possibility.

Cm 46 presumably does not have such a stark view in mind and the critique of the previous paragraph is not meant to imply that the framers of that proposition have such views in mind, but lesser, and perhaps more insidious, versions of such a view can be found in our own society and such views do have to be constrained and regulated. The normal mechanism for such restraint is the Second Declaration of Helsinki which requires the consent of those who are the subjects of medical experiments. The notion of consent, at least in principle, implies that the experiment is carried out on a willing volunteer who has been fully informed of the known effects of the experiment. That principle includes the volunteer, by implication, in the moral community. In other words nothing is being forced upon that person and he or she is being treated not merely as a member of a moral community but also partly as a moral agent in respect of consent, and as a moral subject (or patient) in respect of the experiment.

Insofar as such guidelines are followed strictly and in good faith it seems the bare argument presented in Cm 46 that 'research which could help to alleviate human suffering and handicap has its own moral imperative and justification', fails. Its own moral imperative could and might well permit almost any form of behaviour, would ignore the value of the moral community and the value of membership of that community, and would judge its morality only in terms of benefit. Such an unqualified view of what counts as a moral imperative is sadly lacking in certain crucial respects for it forbids *nothing* if the results appear (probably on extrinsic criteria) to be worthwhile. In practice no responsible experiments are, in fact, carried out without some reference to the Second Declaration of Helsinki which invokes the notion of consent, reasonable knowledge and respect for the subject.

No human (or other) embryo can of course consent, or have reasonable knowledge of the experiment to which it might be subject. Yet it does appear that the embryo, while not an agent, is a moral subject (or patient). No intrinsic criteria have been determined which could reasonably exclude the embryo from, at least passive, membership of the moral community. If that is the case then the embryo is deserving of respect by virtue of that membership and deserves to be treated as an end in itself rather than a means to an end determined by some other. Given these considerations a number of consequences appear to follow.

First, the onus is necessarily placed on those who would exclude certain entities from membership of a moral (or the moral) community to find reasons - other than reasons of convenience - for such an exclusion. We might indeed take a slightly stronger view and argue that inclusion in the moral community (and possibly legal community) should be taken for granted unless compelling evidence is produced to the contrary. In the absence of such evidence we might argue that no one ought to harm or exploit any other entity.

Second, acceptance of the embryo as part of the moral community does invest us with certain obligations towards that embryo - not the least of which is to take care of, and to do what we reasonably can to foster, that being. Our duties, therefore, to such an entity are reasonably clear: namely to take such steps as we can to ensure its well-being and not to subject such a being to any procedure which would harm it and to which it cannot by its nature consent. Any embryonic procedure should, therefore, be limited only to such procedures as might reasonably be expected to promote its individual well-being.

Identity and Individuation

The notions of identity and individuation raise complex philosophical problems which are impossible to fully explore here. Nevertheless they are concepts of some importance to the present discussion. Here the concepts are taken together because there are good philosophical grounds and good practical grounds for doing this. Broadly speaking, we take identity to be that which persists as a whole through time: thus that which has identity maintains that identity not by virtue of some set of descriptions under which it falls, and which predicates completely account for that identity, but rather by some organising principle. Thus any set of descriptions which attach to the entity are mere accidental properties of that object whereas the organising principle could be said to be that which is essential to the identity and to the re-identification of the entity.

Individuation involves the separation of something from its background or from something else. On the view adopted here individuation is always of a 'this such': that is to say, it is an instance of a genus of a certain type. Within the view adopted here, which is broadly Aristotelian, the particular is identified as an instance is individuable, identifiable and re-identifiable. Hence to individuate something which persists through time is to recognise that underlying whatever accidental qualities it might have, it also has some organising principle: its essential properties.

This brief digression into some of the basic principles of individuation is necessary if some marker event, intrinsic to the embryo or zygote, is to be found which would enable us to determine a point at which we could say that there was some qualitative difference between a foetus of a certain age, or stage of development, and a conceptus. As we have seen the Warnock Committee was unable to find such a stage and had to rely on extrinsic, rather than intrinsic criteria, to determine the point of differentiation between 'us' and 'them'. However, some developments since the publication of the Warnock Committee's report have, on some accounts, altered the situation.

The State of Victoria, Australia, in 1984 passed legislation prohibiting certain experiments on human embryos.[14] Underlying that legislation was the view that the human embryo could be distinguished by virtue of its individuation. In 1986, Wood and Rogers, two scientists working in the area of embryonic research submitted a proposal which sought the permission of the Standing Review and Advisory Committee to create forty embryos which would be microsurgically inseminated with human sperm. Wood and Rogers argued that as individuation took place only after syngamy (literally the marriage or fusion of two cells or nuclie in reproduction) their research would not fall into the category of prohibited research. Syngamy takes place somewhere between 20 and 22 hours after conception and by destroying the cells before syngamy, Wood and Rogers hoped to escape the penalties of the Infertility Medical Procedures Act of 1894.

By challenging the Act in this way, Wood and Rogers hoped to show that there was a distinct marker event, namely syngamy, before which an embryo could not be individuated. If the embryo could not be individuated, it was argued, it was not deserving of moral and legal respect. What is interesting about this particular case is not merely that an Act of Parliament no matter how carefully drafted can be challenged in such a way, but that the two scientists involved by so challenging it accepted that individuation was an important moral (and legal) milestone in the development of a human being. In other words, individuation was crucial to the development of a particular human being. Morally, if not legally, Wood and Rogers implicitly accepted that the criteria of individuation was crucial.

Biologically, Wood and Rogers' argument, though ingenious, is mistaken. At the moment of conception, the individuality of the particular gametes is lost in favour of a new individual entity. That entity can be individuated whereas the gametes can no longer be said to possess the individuality that they once had. At the moment of conception the entire genetic pattern for a new individual is laid down. That genetic pattern will, if allowed to develop, produce a unique human life, which with the exception of twins, is quite unlike any other human being. That individual is not only unique but is identifiable and re-identifiable. The same considerations apply to identical twins which though genetically identical are, in accordance with Leibniz's law, separately identifiable and re-identifiable. The medical evidence is similarly uncontroversial. In summarising the evidence of expert witnesses a New Zealand Inquiry put the issue succintly:

> From a biological point of view there is no argument as to when life begins. Evidence was given to us from eminent scientists from all over the world. None of them suggested that human life begins at any time other than conception.[15]

But it is not just that conception is the point at which a new and unique human life has begun, it is also the point at which the fundamental organising principle for that life is laid down. Hence an individual, in the sense outlined above, is brought into being. That individual is not just a set of accidental properties which can be brought under a description. It is not just a cluster of properties and cannot be described merely as a set of predicates. Underlying those surface properties is an organising principle which can be said to constitute, in the terms that we have used, the essential properties without which the organism would not be what it was but would be either nothing (or if the organising principle were something else) would be another individual. It seems as if there is no 'marker event' beyond conception which would avoid Somerville's concerns.

The Initial Argument Restated

Part of the Warnock report, Cm 46 and Cm 259, is addressed to the question of surrogacy. This is not a question with which we have been directly concerned. Nevertheless there is one point which interests us. That point is the Government's intention to make the carrying mother, in any surrogacy arrangement, the legal mother. The Government proposes to make surrogacy arrangements unenforceable and hence the genetic parents will not be the legal parents should the carrying, or surrogacy, mother so object.

On the face of it this might seem to be a strange doctrine. At first sight it would seem that the donors of the gametes would have some claim their own genetic material. Ostensibly the Government's reason for this move is to extend the discouragement of surrogacy arrangements. There is, however, a further implication to such an arrangement. By denying the donors of gametes a claim on those gametes, it becomes clear that in law, and probably in ethics, there is an underlying intention to treat the genetic material of a donor as property. In law it will be clear that neither the genetic material, nor any human embryo or individual produced as a result of the donation and fusion of such gametes, will be the property of the genetic donors.

This decision suggests to us that the only ethical model appropriate to the embryo (or fused gametes) is not one of ownership, or of property, but one of stewardship or guardianship. A concrete example might help in understanding this view. In 1984, two Australians visiting South America were killed in a 'plane crash. The couple, Mario and Elsa Rios had been treated for infertility by I.V.F. and had left a fertilised ovum in deep freeze. Were the normal laws of property and inheritance to apply then the frozen ovum would have been destroyed or its disposal left to the estate. Neither course of action was taken. The decision was taken by those maintaining the frozen ovum to thaw it and to implant it into another woman.[16] The decision was taken without regard to the estate. The clear implication was that the holders of the ovum regarded themselves as the stewards or guardians of the embryo and did not regard the embryo as property to be disposed of in the normal manner. We maintain that deliberate or not, this steward or guardian model is a clear ethical implication of the Government's present decision and that such a model is indeed appropriate for embryos. The embryo is not property, it is a moral subject, held in our trust as part of the moral community. As such it is a moral subject or patient until such time as it assumes full powers of agency.

It should be clear from the foregoing argument that we regard the embryo as a moral subject deserving of respect and that we regard the conceptus as an individual identifiable and re-identifiable with an intrinsic organisation oriented towards a human and social future. Within that context some of our initial arguments which may have seemed at first sight puzzling may now make sense. In restating those arguments hopefully the position that they represent will now be clear.

We took it that:

b) the basis of human life has some moral claim upon us,

an argument that can be justified from our concern to and for the future;

c) the genetic basis of human life is not itself a person,

an argument that can be understood from our conception of what counts as a person. Nevertheless we took it that the genetic basis of human life is an individual, identifiable and re-identifiable which is organised according to some fundamental principle and oriented towards a human and social future. It followed that while we regarded the conceptus as deserving of the utmost respect that we could not accept that part of Cm 259 or Cm 46 which simply equated zygocide with homicide and which we expressed as,

d) the destruction of a conceptus or zygote is not tantamount to homicide.

However, we could find no case for experimentation on moral subjects who could not, or did not, consent to such experimentation. Any claim to benefit did not outweigh this view, hence,

e)...the destruction of a zygote....is not warranted by some mere (putative) or informed claim to benefit.

Nor could we find that research to alleviate human suffering had its own moral imperative. Indeed we found that claim to be extremely dangerous. Any claim of such a kind would need to be supported by arguments external to itself and which showed that human beings would be treated as ends in themselves and not as mere means. Hence,

f)...the claim that 'research which could help to alleviate human suffering and handicap has its own moral imperative and justification...' is not self sufficient.

Therefore, we can accept the claim in S. 51 of Cm 46 that the view that 'the embryo should, from the point of conception, be regarded as having the same full human status as the child is misplaced' while denying that 'research which could help to alleviate human suffering and handicap has its own moral imperative and justification'. The conclusion we reach, therefore, is that the arguments of S. 51 do not 'support embryo research' and that on its own terms those arguments fail.

We would instead adopt the model which is also implied in the Government's firm proposals that the embryo is not property and that the property model is not appropriate to this realm of human life. Indeed we would go so far as to suggest that the Government's proposals would be deeply contradictory should they permit, on the one hand, procedures which were not designed to protect and safeguard the embryo in experimental situations while, simultaneously on the other hand, adopting an implied guardianship or trusteeship model. It is perhaps to the least of us and to the weakest of us that the greatest care is required.

In the following chapter, a principle claim made from a political and philosophical perspective, that the weak may be deserving of restraint of the exercise of power from the strong, is given a theological basis.

3

THEOLOGY AND ETHICS

In this chapter we explore some of the theological dimensions to the question of research on embryos. Interestingly, we find that a mainstream theological argument supports and complements the political and philosophical arguments of the preceding chapter. We reach the conclusion that the arguments developed in the first two chapters, though beginning from different standpoints, one secular, the other theological, converge to produce a surprising unity of perspective. In the following chapter, that unity of perspective is shown to underpin the submission that we made to the Government in mid 1987. It should be clear, therefore, that this submission though not explicitly expressing the underlying philosophical and theological perspectives, does nevertheless implicitly contain those perspectives.

The Least Among Us

'Truly, I say to you, as you did it to one of the least of these my brethren, you did it to me.' Such is the reply of Jesus, as recorded by Matthew, to 'the righteous' who expect eternal life.[1] The parable as a whole and Jesus' interpretation of it, is a remarkable challenge to the narrowness of moral concern exemplified by the ruling religious elite of the time. Matthew's account is sometimes challenged, especially by Jewish scholars, who claim that parts of the Gospels present a caricature of Jewish sects - such as the Pharisees - or even actually misrepresent their true teaching. But even allowing for this possibility, there can be no dispute about the general position advocated by Jesus at this point: He is at pains to extend the fullness of moral obligation even to those who in his own society possessed reduced or diminished moral standing.

> I was hungry and you gave me food, I was thirsty and you gave me drink, I was a stranger and you welcomed me, I was naked and you clothed me, I was sick and you visited me, I was in prison and you came to me.[2]

Prison visiting in our time is for some at least a commonplace occurrence. Some may argue about the effectiveness or the appropriateness of this practice but few, perhaps very few, would not see it is morally righteous. But at the time of Christ, there was no more hated and dreaded a person than one who was a criminal. Terrible penalties were inflicted upon captives, as Jesus himself was soon to discover. If released, a captive became an immediate social outcast. Again feeding the hungry or giving drink to the thirsty or visiting the sick are not nowadays exceptional activities. Indeed, thanks to the teaching of Jesus, it would be thought to be scandalous that any religious person could be 'Christian' at all without engaging in such practices. We need to remember, however, that at the time of Jesus, the hungry begged on the streets, the sick - far from being visited - were banished to small collectives and ostracised as a matter of course. The diseased, captive and dying had no Hospice movement, no penal reform lobby and no welfare system to defend them. They were, quite literally, out on their own. Religious people could be righteous, and what is more, be seen to be righteous, without lifting a finger to help those socially disadvantaged in their society.

The Moral Priority of the Weak

Viewed from this perspective, the attitude of Jesus is nothing less than shocking. He does not simply commend charitable works in a way that indicates how all circumstances being equal (since of course they never are for those who are really disadvantaged) we should help those who are worse off. Rather he makes care for the outcast a test of religiosity, and therefore of true righteousness. Indeed nothing less than his whole personal authority before God is at stake in the way the question is posed and answered:

> for I was hungry and you gave me no food, I was thirsty and you gave me no drink, I was a stranger and you gave me no drink, I was a stranger and you did not clothe me, sick and in prison you did not visit me. Then they will answer, 'Lord when we did see thee hungry or thirsty or a stranger or naked or sick or in prison, and did not minister to thee?'[3]

This absolute identification of the moral claims of Christ, and by implication of God himself, with those of suffering, disadvantaged humanity would be striking enough simply as one parabolic episode of the Gospel of St. Matthew. But in fact what we find here is one single and consistent strand throughout all the Gospels. In Mark's Gospel, Jesus commends the way of sacrificial loving that is to become the hallmark of his disciples,[4] in John's Gospel, Jesus washes the dirty feet of his apostles and sets them an example which they are to manifest to the world,[5] and in Luke's Gospel, the very beginning of Jesus' ministry begins with his bold identification with the words of Isaiah:

> The Spirit of the Lord is upon me, because he has anointed me to preach good news to the poor. He has sent me to proclaim release to the captives and the recovery of sight to the blind, to set at liberty those who are oppressed, to proclaim the acceptable year of the Lord.[6]

If we are to take this strand of the Gospels seriously, therefore, we are led to the disturbing thought not only that the vulnerable and the oppressed ought to command our moral concern, but also that Jesus himself actually gives moral priority to those who are the 'least of all'. Slowly but surely New Testament expositors, are beginning to grapple with this disturbing aspect of the Gospel itself. David Sheppard, Bishop of Liverpool, completes his book *Bias to the Poor* with the challenging question 'Can the Church Bear Good News to the Poor?' and his own answer is often less than sanguine.[7] Again, Charles Elliott, recently Director of Christian Aid, argues that praying the kingdom requires 'standing in all our weakness before God on the side of the poor, and offering our psychic energies in the great battle against evil in ourselves, in our environment and in the whole cosmos'.[8]

But the question has to be asked: Who *are* the least of all - at least in the human community of 'brethren' apparently assumed here by Jesus? We know that the parable of the sheep and the goats was, amongst other things, an attack upon the narrowness of moral concern displayed by so many religious of his time. But the point of the ethical teaching is not just that such and such a category of persons which had previously been excluded should now be included within our field of moral concern, such as prisoners, the hungry and the sick, but that *all* human beings whenever and wherever they are despised and rejected and suffering should be the regarded as having a prior claim upon us.

If this teaching was difficult at the time of Jesus, it is not less difficult today. Whilst to some kinds of human beings, such as the poor, the hungry and perhaps even prisoners, we are arguably more charitable than our religious forebears, it is also the case that our society is still governed by multifarious 'utilitarian' criteria of the worth of human beings. We still speak, and sometimes act, negatively about those kinds of human beings, for example, who are thought not to do enough work, or those who are mentally enfeebled, or those who have been born with certain cultural and racial characteristics. In other words, while we may relieve ourselves of *some* charges against the weak and vulnerable today, we are hardly free of that indifference or even hostility to those claims of individual human beings who are conventionally thought of as 'less' than us.

The Moral Status of the Embryo

The question of the status of embryos and their use in scientific research is a case in point. For what can be more vulnerable than pre-birth life? If we are to locate the weakest of all in our present society, those individuals who are most incapable of defending themselves or preventing their own harm or destruction, it is difficult to envisage any one single category of human beings that are more consistently both weak and defenceless than unborn human beings.

And yet so little are unborn humans regarded, that their very 'leastness' has been turned into an argument *against* respecting them. For some, perhaps many, will complain that unborn human beings are *not* actually human beings at all. Even some Christian arguments are used in ways that undermine the status of unborn life. There are three in particular that we have already isolated.

Embryos as Potential Humans

The first is that unborn human life is 'potentially human life' but not actual human life and therefore undeserving of the full status that we should give to adult humans. The Board for Social Responsibility of the Church of England in its evidence to the DHSS Report of the Committee of Enquiry argued that:

> The majority of us however believe that modern embryology enables us to make a judgement of value and believe that (on the view that the more probable view should prevail) until the embryo has reached the first 14 days of its existence, it is not yet entitled to the same respect and protection as an embryo implanted in the human womb and in which individualisation has begun.[9]

Unsoulled Humans

The second is that embryos are 'unformed' or as yet 'unsoulled' individual humans. Once the link is made between the possession of human soulfulness and the faculty of reason (and necessarily consciousness as well) it is not surprising that embryos who are clearly devoid of these capacities should be regarded as unsoulled or 'soul-less'. This view has strong Scholastic support of various kinds. It is well known that St. Thomas Aquinas held that the rational soul was not instilled into the body until 40 days after conception. By making this distinction it was possible to make a further distinction between 'foeticide' and 'homicide'. 'During this period abortion of the unformed foetus was condemned but was not considered to be homicide'.[10]

Embryos as Non-persons

The third is that embryos are not 'persons' in the sense that full humanhood requires. 'It is important not to suggest that human beings must exercise some specific degree of intelligence or emotional maturity before they can be regarded as human persons', warns the Report of a Working Party of the Board for Social Responsibility. 'Yet', it maintains, 'if we are to draw a morally relevant distinction between humans and other animals, we seem compelled to define the human in terms of a sort of nature able to exercise rational, moral and personal capacities'.[11] Since this nature is insufficiently developed in embryonic human life, it follows that the claim of embryos to moral status cannot be equal to that of adult humans.

According to all three views, therefore, what is the moral status of the embryo? The conclusion which all three appear to come to is as follows:

> We believe it to be consistent with this Anglican tradition to hold that, while a fertilised ovum should be treated with respect, its life is not so sacrosanct that it should be accorded the same status as we

afford to human beings.[12]

The procedure inherent in all three perspectives involves the isolating of one or more 'morally relevant' distinctions which lead inexorably to the diminishing of moral status. Each distinction does not stand alone of course. The notion of 'soulfulness' is clearly fed by the corresponding notion of the value of adult 'maturity' or subject 'consciousness'. All these distinctions have been criticised and the criticisms have taken various forms. It is possible, for example, to insist upon the 'continuity of the individual subject' as one of the Reports emphasises.[13] It is also possible to question the use of criteria such as 'rationality' which is, after all, only a variable, and some have boldly admitted that the difference between unborn and just - born rationality is hardly significant.[14] It is also possible to dispute each view with the assertion that all *innocent* human life however differentiated requires, even demands, our protection in accordance with the command to respect human life.[15]

Drawing the Line

And yet despite these criticisms, it seems difficult to deny that all three views are cogent enough in their own terms. *If* moral status depends wholly upon the attribution of certain qualities or capacities, then surely these arguments have strength as well as coherence. We may quibble about the terms or definitions or extent of these attributes but if moral status is actually tied to them, then the debate even between those for or against experimentation, if conducted in these terms, are only questions about where we draw the line. One of the Anglican Reports admits as much. In answering the 'understandable' fear that experimentation on early embryos may lead to experimentation on full human subjects, it argues that the 'answer to the argument is to point out that we all have to draw the line somewhere, whether it is at conception or later'.[16]

It seems to us that an entirely different kind of criticism should be levelled at all three arguments. Such a critique begins by taking seriously the idea enshrined in the Gospels that the weaker have a greater claim upon us. How far, if at all, such an argument can be extended outside the human community is another question and one of us has sought to discuss in another context.[17] But whatever the arguments about the claims of lions and elephants, few Christians would deny that it is the human community of persons who are singled out by Jesus in the Matthean parable to which we have already referred. We need to remind ourselves that the poor, the sick, the diseased and the captive represented in Jesus' own time, and later, the very categories or human subjects who were thought to possess minimal moral standing. The scandal of this is not reduced when we consider the instances of Jesus associating with the whole range of those who were feared as 'unclean', especially the diseased, the sexually impure, the hated tax-collectors and the demonically possessed. The logic employed by Matthew appears to be that the 'higher' should sacrifice themselves for the 'lower' and not the reverse. In other words, the ethical teaching of Jesus is directed at the *widening* of moral sensitivity rather than at its diminution or channelling into narrow, sectional concerns. Even the demands of the family (an esteemed institution then as now in Judaism) are to be subservient to the demands of the Gospel.[18]

Now, we do not pretend that the demands of this teaching are other than considerable. Like most that is authentically Jesus, the way is costly and demanding. But it is authentically Christian - at least as authentic as the many other voices within Christendom - in that it judges the worth of human subjects not by conventional human standards but by the love of God expressed in Jesus Christ. For it cannot be gainsaid that the fascinating quality of the ethical demands of Jesus rely in turn upon the irreducibility of the moral worth of human creation in the sight of God. This moral worth, theologically founded, does not simply extend to those who are 'innocent' or 'pure' or who have social position or reputation. It encompasses *at least* all human beings whether they are sinful or righteous, ugly or beautiful, free or captive, religious or heathen. But it finds its special focus, its enduring point in the championing of the vulnerable, the despised and the weak. 'Jesus himself', writes T. W. Manson, is the standing example of the attitude which 'he demands of his followers'.

> It is no accident that he is called 'the friend of publicans and sinners' - the lover of the unlovely and the unlovable. His own ideal of divine love, which is the pattern for human love, is portrayed for us in the father of the prodigal and the elder brother: we must remember that neither the selfish libertine who went abroad nor the cantankerous prig who stayed at home is an amiable type of character. Nevertheless the father goes out to meet them both: and as the father is, so must men be who aspire to be his children.[19]

Arguments against: (i) Individualist Ethics

Exegesis of the Gospel in these terms does not go unchallenged. Four arguments in particular are brought against any attempt to bring this aspect of the Gospel message into the field of social ethics.

The first objection, holds that Gospel ethics of this kind are essentially individualistic, appropriate, even commendable, for individual human action, but inappropriate, even disastrous, when applied to social intercourse. Jesus, we are assured, was giving illustrations of the kind of ethical motivation which should inspire his individual followers but only as individuals. It is well known that the ethical teaching of Jesus goes far beyond concern with mere behaviour as such and encompasses a whole range of qualities such as attitude, disposition and motivation, and how therefore, it is argued, can we make these the subject of social regulations or indeed collective legislation?

This objection seems a strong one. We do well not to rush from every prescription found in scripture to the view that each of these should properly or wisely be embodied in social regulation and law. It is also true that we should make some effort to understand the nature of Jesus' teaching in its historical context and try to distinguish as far as possible what may apply to whom and in what circumstances. Very few churchpeople, in our experience, have, for example, taken Jesus literally at his word when it comes to turning one's cheek or running another mile or not refusing anything that is asked of one.[20] But because we need to distinguish the different kinds of ethical teaching given by Jesus and because we may well be right in regarding, for example, the teaching of the Sermon on the Mount as laying foundational ideals for the Christian life rather than offering a clear set of duties - these considerations should not blind us to the contours of his teaching even if we may be lacking many of the details. Accordingly we do not base our argument on any one text by itself but appeal to one varied, but consistent strand, within the New Testament itself. Moreover, it is when we look to the life of Jesus as a whole: its self-sacrifice, its moral generosity and its fidelity to a God who is himself unconditionally generous that we can fully appreciate the traditional claim that generous, forgiving love is at the heart of the universe.

But how can we claim this generous loving as the hallmark of Christian discipleship without trying to live out this life with others? Doubtless there are things we need to do as individuals to make the vision clear or to live more peaceably. But it is difficult to avoid the conclusion that Jesus is as much concerned with our social relations as with our individual piety, if not more so. Are not questions about how we treat the sick, the dying, the diseased and the poor as much social questions today as they were in the time of Jesus? Now it is true that Jesus did not, as far as we can see, legislate on social issues in a simple, straightforward manner. We look in vain in the New Testament for a political manifesto. But it is an impoverishment of the Gospel to suggest that the moral attitudes and behaviour commended by Jesus should be relegated to the personal, private world of individual religiosity.

But some may surely question: Can the greater claim of the weak realistically be embodied in law? Is not it enough that individuals try as best they can to live generous lives? Is not legislation an inappropriate tool for personal, let alone 'social' holiness? This argument has force. Legislation of any kind, social, civic or ecclesiastical, has profound moral limits. Law cannot make us morally righteous, and Jesus helps us see the deficiency of moral obligation construed solely in legal terms. As Manson suggests:

> Jesus is chiefly concerned with the heart of man as the spring of conduct rather than with the Law as the regulative force in society. [21]

All this can be accepted and yet it can still be that the proper function of law is to defend the defenceless. Indeed on a Christian reading it may be that the best, even only, satisfactory justification for law is precisely this: that the preciousness of what God has given should be safeguarded and that the weak should not be exploited. Now we accept, of course, that on the relationship between Christian ethics and social legislation many legitimate views can be held. All we would want to defend here is that it is as arguably a Christian view of the function of legislation that it should give priority to defending the weak and the vulnerable as is the contrary view that legislation should maximise the freedom of the strong. The argument here of course is far from novel. Early in the history of ancient Israel we find prophets contending against oppression, defending the fatherless and pleading for the widow.[22] Arguably Jesus stands within this same prophetic tradition which insists upon social justice as one criterion of personal righteousness.

Arguments against: (ii) The Need to Compromise

The second objection, common to Christian and non-Christian alike, is that giving priority to the weak is largely impractical. All human arrangements, it is argued, are matters of negotiation. It is inevitable that the strong should take advantage of the weak. Moreover in the complex world in which we live moral compromise and accommodation in all matters are essential if we are to refrain from electing heroism or even martyrdom.

Some may doubt whether this view is ever held in the crass form in which it is expounded here, but we have heard some actually defend it in an even stronger form, and conceivably some, perhaps many, have real sympathy for it. Some Christians are apt to write off this argument as devoid of any moral content, but they are mistaken. It is fed from a variety of perceptions. It is true, after all, that the strong invariably do exploit the weak and that, as Thrasymacus contended, 'might is right' - if not as a general rule - then certainly in many contexts in which we live today. Moreover, there can be a naivety in which Christians contend for the oppressed and the underprivileged in ways which appear to show little regard for the realities of power. But the question that must be confronted is whether by allowing estimates of the worth and utility of other human beings, derived largely from social and economic factors, to dominate our perception of the common good we provide a satisfactory basis even for the protection of the strong. For such is the world of Jesus - and our world too - that anyone can become weak through illness, disease or injury and almost anyone can, through unforeseen circumstances, become poor or vulnerable or both. It is a solipsism that postulates eternal freedom from disadvantage.

Moreover, such considerations have real force when we relate them to the status of unborn human life and to the threat of institutionalised experimentation. Given that we know how difficult it is for habits of advantage to be dismantled and given that individuals who cannot claim for themselves are frequently marginalised, we do well to ponder before legalising an institutional practice which, however lofty its aims, can in practice overlook the moral status of its experimental subjects. If it is true that there is an inbuilt tendency on the part of the strong to infringe the claims of the weak, we need to reflect how the least among us can be properly defended. Of course the defence of the weak can impose heavy burdens upon the strong; the capacity to desist from activities to our own advantage or to the advantage of others, is always precarious. But if we are to speak of the realities of power, the question may well be: Who is to have the prior claim given that the strong invariably have the advantage?

Arguments against: (iii) Unacceptable consequences

The third objection is that to adopt a moral position in favour of the weak involves us in morally unacceptable consequences. If we grant a higher claim to the weak, for example the embryo or the foetus, we shall as a matter of principle oppose all abortions even in those cases where the life and well-being of the mother is at stake. If the price to be paid for support of the weak is an absolutist position on abortion then that price is simply too high.

The first point that must be made in reply to this objection is that the competing claims of the mother versus the foetus, if it comes to this, do need to be weighed. It cannot be accepted as axiomatic that every claim against the unborn child is necessarily a prior one. But whatever view is held about the morality of abortion in certain limited situations, it should be quite clear that the ethical issue posed by the proposed legislation of experimentation on embryos is different in a number of significant respects. To hold as a general principle that the weak should have priority over the strong cannot absolve us from the difficulty in deciding between competing claims in particular instances. Even allowing for our bias towards the weak, we have to acknowledge that in particular circumstances judgements may vary. Some may consistently hold that even allowing for our principle, the mother's claim to life must take priority over that of an unborn child especially where other dependents are involved. The case for the weak, it may be argued, requires our support for the strong. But, it must be noted, that in this case and in similar ones, we are at least faced with a choice between *directly* competing claims. As our submission shows,[23] no such claim can reasonably be made in the area of experimentation on human embryos. By refusing to experiment, we do no direct harm; we injure no-one and infringe no rights. It is vital to distinguish between those cases where we are genuinely faced with a moral dilemma and those cases where we are faced with a choice between a direct harm and a hypothetical benefit.

It is here that we touch upon one of the most disturbing aspects of Anglican discussions on the use of embryos in research. They simply take over from the Warnock Committee itself the general claim that research offers 'benefits' of an unspecified kind without asking the central moral question whether such 'benefits' are of such an order as to justify (even within their own terms) the destruction of embryos who are supposed to qualify for 'special protection' and 'respect' for life.[24] The lack of critical judgement in this area is astonishing, since the whole claim for the use of embryos in research crucially hangs - even in utilitarian terms - upon what kinds of benefit can be said to accrue from experimentation. In the various arguments adduced in favour of the destruction of embryonic life we need to be aware that we are not presented with one example of serious or significant benefit where failure to experiment offers us anything like a direct choice between 'evils'. It is not surprising that some who register caution at this point wonder whether the unspecified but seductive claims of 'progress' and 'research' are not claiming a priority above concerns for human life itself. For if vacuous claims for 'benefit' can render the moral status of the embryo to the point where it can be destroyed at will, we may indeed question whether the logic of this position does not in fact require experimentation upon adult humans - the use of which, we shall be assured, will accrue even greater 'benefit'.

But the argument concerning 'benefit', even if allowed within its own terms, cannot stand sufficiently as a defensible theological argument in favour of experimentation on embryos. Even if it could be shown that experimentation on embryos brought immediate benefits to other humans, it would still be wrong to destroy individual embryos for that purpose. It is inconceivable that the tradition which holds all human life to be precious in the sight of God could justify on theological grounds the use of some forms of this God-given life as little more than resources for our benefit. Even embryos which according to the majority Anglican view have a diminished moral status still have in their own terms a claim that outweighs the vacuous claims to human 'benefit'. We should be clear that to experiment on early human life is a procedure involving nothing less than the destruction of genetically unique individuals. It is disingenuous or 'Newspeak', to talk of 'respecting' the life of an embryo which has such little standing that it can be utilised and destroyed as nothing more than a laboratory resource.

To argue in this fashion is not to impugn the integrity of scientists some of which undoubtedly hold that the use of embryos would offer long-term benefits to human society. It would be wrong to polarise the discussion in terms of 'scientists' and 'us'. But it has to be asked whether the scientific community is well served by its almost automatic defence of research and whether moral decisions which concern all citizens can be properly left to scientists. If we are to appeal to unspecified claims for 'benefit' to society as a whole then we are also justified in appealing to other no *less* tangible factors such as the cumulative effects of disrespect for human life. There is a balance to be weighed even at this indirect distance: we simply do not know the long-term effects of the routinised and institutionalised use of unborn humans in scientific investigation. We may not be in a position to calculate its results, positive or negative, for society as a whole. The very unpredictable and hypothetical nature of the evidence must tell *against* their use.

Arguments against: (iv) Taking Power for God

The fourth objection is to our mind an altogether more sophisticated and important one. It draws its strength from two deeply held theological ideas: the concept of 'human dominion' on one hand and the idea that creation is as yet 'unfinished' on the other. In the third Report - without doubt most thorough Anglican contribution to this subject so far - we are invited to reflect upon certain questions relating to 'what our view of nature is':

> is it a realm whose limits are set unchangeably, or a world in process perhaps towards an as yet unrealised goal? Secondly, what is our view of the relation of nature and God's purpose - has He set purposes in nature, which we ought not to frustrate, or are we free, or indeed have a duty, to shape nature towards the realisation of a moral goal? And thirdly, what is our view of the limits of human responsibility - are we bound to respect the natural order of things, just as it is, or is nature a morally neutral order upon which we may impose what we perceive to be good purposes? [25]

These questions are surely a welcome relief from the usually narrow and sometimes moribund terms in which the debate about unborn life is frequently couched. The Report has provided an opportunity for

Christians to begin the important task of recognising the important differences of theological perspective and interpretation that lie behind this ethical issue as they do behind many others. We might wish that more Church Reports gave themselves over to this important work of clarification and understanding so that Christians themselves might understand the varied and contrasting ethical possibilities that arise out of their own tradition. Our understanding of nature, either as a fixed entity or as a developing process or as in some ways both, can crucially affect our perception of the values within it. If dominion means that we are given power to co-operate with God, and if it is the case that the world is as yet radically unfinished, then:

> we cannot simply look for the preservation of human nature as it has been, as though perfection was in the past, and all change must be degeneration. Instead, we need to think how the world should be and how we can either protect its integrity or realise its God-given possibilities so as to advance towards the realisation of God's purpose.[26]

This is well put. And if this view is adopted it might well be possible to argue, as the majority of the Working Group did, that interference in the early life of humans can be justifiable in the hope that it secures a better world and the fulfilment of God's purposes. The conclusion of the majority view, in supporting the legislation of experiments on embryos up to 14 days old, was that as part of our responsible dominion 'we have a duty to judge when, in the development of a human life, a particular life has reached a stage where it possesses the essential features of the full human being and therefore must be protected'.[27]

It would be an inadequate response to this argument to hold that 'all nature is good' or that 'every structure within nature is God-given'. There is, we do well to remind ourselves, a great deal of parasitism and violence within the natural order itself. It seems to us that the view that creation is as yet unfinished, judged by the standards of the Prince of Peace at least, is difficult to dispute. Accepting that point however, still leaves us with the enormous difficulty in postulating that the process towards the realisation of God's will for creation involves, indeed necessitates, the utilisation of methods which actually involves us in the destruction of precious individuals within that God-given creation itself. Now it is true that all human life as we know it involves the making of painful choices and sometimes the acceptance of what is sometimes called the 'lesser evil' - though some of us would have reservations about the use of that term. But it is surely one thing to say that God so creates a world in which moral accommodation and compromise are sometimes inevitable given the world as it is and given the sinful character of human beings, and quite another to say that God actually advances his perfectly good will through these accommodations and compromises. Doubtless God's will is mysterious and somehow God does make the best even of the worst things that human beings sometimes do. As T. F. Torrance observes, though God is frequently frustrated, he continues to work in and through the frustration of his creatures.[28] But it is surely difficult to postulate the perfect-like purposes of an almighty loving God who actually requires of us to use our power in ways that infringe the interests of the weak. It is commonplace to observe that totalitarian regimes either of the right or of the left are apt to justify the sufferings of their subjects in the present for the sake of the glorious future that is to come. Is God really so desperate, we may ask, that he requires his creatures to do the same?

The difficulty then with this underlying theological perspective - that justifies the destruction of embryos for the sake of divine purpose - does not consist in its notion of process and change but in its definition of what could be in accordance with the purpose of a holy, loving deity. Nature *may* in some sense be morally neutral. It may be that we are destined to be freer of 'natural constraints' in our moral as well as in our physical lives than we had previously supposed in our history. All these things may well be. 'We are in the midst of a journey', maintains the Report, 'whose beginnings lay in creation and whose end is to be realised in the hope given to us in Jesus Christ'. Again the point is finely put. But what is the 'hope' given to us in Jesus Christ? What kind of hope could it be that justifies the oppression of the weak and the vindication of the strong? What could be good about the news of the

Prince of Peace who actually endorses - what many in fact deeply fear in their darkest moments - namely that the value of human life is defined by those who have the advantage and the power to destroy it.

The Realities of Power

For if Christians have been regrettably naive about the realities of power in the past then we do well to attend to the realities of power in the issue of experimentation on embryos. Let us make no mistake: those that define unborn life as no 'real' human life are precisely those who support, advocate or actually practice this destruction of life at the present time. The status of the embryo is not some interesting byway of moral speculation. It is a practical issue thrown up by the very fact that the status of embryos has to be defined now in the light of current procedures. No matter how good or honourable the intentions of scientists, we must be clear that the *institutionalisation* of any experimental practice can easily lead to accustomed indifference. Those who doubt this need to learn from the institutionalised practice of animal experimentation. Despite welfare legislation, advisory committees, full time inspectors and active public concern, one distinguished scientist with a lifetime's experience in the laboratory is able to lament:

> Looking back at the first half of my life as a zoologist I am particularly impressed by one fact: none of the teachers, lecturers, or professors with whom I came into contact - and that includes my kindly father - none of the directors of laboratories where I worked, and none of my co-workers, ever discussed with me, or each other in my presence, *the ethics of zoology*. Nor did they ask me what I was trying to do, what were my zoological aims and aspirations, and in what framework I saw the life-cycles I was elucidating. No one ever suggested that one should respect the lives of animals in the laboratory or that they, and not the experiments, however fascinating and instructive, were worthy of greater consideration.[30]

We shall be told, of course, that it will be different with human subjects - that scientists will work with even greater care and scrupulosity. That may indeed be so. But we have to remind ourselves that even the most sensitive scientist can become desensitised through habitualised practice - especially when the experiments themselves have become routine and when the practice of asking awkward questions about the experimental subjects themselves, as Miriam Rothschild graphically indicates, has long since ceased. We have to ask how practically possible it will be, in the light of experience itself, to defend the interests of human subjects in the laboratory when even now controlling legislation in the field of animal experimentation still permits of excesses and indifference - despite the best will in the world and even the most noble of motives. Retrospective or 'reactive' legislation invariably works against those whose interests are currently being infringed by the powerful for the simple reason that habits of life are not easily changed, even by regulation. This is not to suppose that scientists are blissfully unaware of all their social responsibilities; neither is it to suppose a scientific conspiracy determined to undermine the value of human life. The actual situation strikes us as infinitely less grand and actually more sinister. It is of well-meaning people who in their absolute commitment to pursue what they regard as a legitimate good practically overlook the moral status of their research subjects. They want, in other words, to draw the line in a different place (as we all invariably do) to legitimise what they are already in fact doing.

Dominion and Despotism

This fourth objection we have seen also makes use of the notion of 'human dominion' over nature. The use of this term may be more unfortunate than its users imagine. In the first place 'dominion' has in many moral situations with the non-human itself become a byword for 'despotism' rather than responsible use. The history of our treatment of animals shows clearly how the advantage of power has been turned almost without thinking into the abuse of power.[31] We now appreciate, of course, that 'dominion' is misinterpreted when it is employed to justify exploitation. If anything, it suggests in context something altogether more grand like a global commission to make and maintain God's peace within creation.[32]

But it should also be clear that human dominion in God's enveloping creation has necessarily a dynamic quality to it. 'Christians may say that the discovery of new possibilities is an aspect of God's providential care', argues the Report, 'and that, whatever our judgements on particular developments, we ought not to fear new things'.[33] This warning seems to be appropriate. If the Spirit is to lead us in to 'all the truth'[34] then at the very least we ought to be prepared to revise our received opinions or prejudices from time to time. If the God of Jesus Christ is also the God of the future, we must expect to learn new things. But if we are to respect what is to be given in the future, it is also vital that we do not let go of anything precious in the present. There is a dialectical quality to faithful living: receiving the past and being open to the present. To sharpen the issue a little further: the 'goods' in creation must not then be sacrificed to some 'greater good' promised us for the future. If we do not hold onto this, we shall be led to little more than projecting onto God the utilitarian estimations that seduce us from generation to generation. We must test, in other words, both what is given and what is promised. If a modicum of scepticism is permitted, it must be allowed play both ways. If to take the case in point, we are unsure about the precise status of the embryo, we should be equally unsure about the imprecise benefits claimed by those who would destroy them.

Jesus and Powerlessness

One of the 'six principles' enumerated by the Report for understanding developments in modern technology concerns 'Jesus Christ and the Divine Purpose'. What can be known by reference to Jesus about the nature of the divine purpose?

> There is so much to be gained by studying His teaching, His miracles, His person as described in the New Testament, His authority and His action on and in the world, and especially His death and resurrection. In particular we learn from him the worth and dignity of human life, of the depth of possibilities for human relationships and of interdependent social life as represented for example in the notion of the church as the 'body of Christ'.[35]

But there is also one further quite critically relevant thing that we can also learn - not just from one or two lines in the New Testament- but from the whole character and life of Jesus as interpreted by the early church. It is that the life of God in our world is one of service. Even more: that the omnipotence and power of God in his incarnate life is expressed in humility, condescension (*katabasis*) and sacrificial loving. When we ask, therefore, what it means for his disciples to have power, there can be for Christians only one proper answer or rather model to follow. It is nothing less than the one who is, as St. Paul puts it, 'the power of God' on earth.[36] If the power of God is expressed in powerlessness, that is in sharing the suffering of the weak, then we have to qualify every claim made for human dominion which does not explicitly accept this Christological paradigm.

Even, indeed especially, here where the Report hopes to find comfort in the notion of man's God-given freedom over the earth, we find that freedom is actually defined in the Gospels in terms that turn our usual meaning of that notion upside down. 'The kings of the Gentiles exercise lordship over them; and those in authority over them are called benefactors', records St. Luke. 'But not so with you; rather let the greatest among you become as the youngest, and the leader as one who serves'.[37] The logic of Jesus, here as everywhere, is hard. However we may interpret these verses, they cannot reasonably be claimed as providing a new warrant for the interests of the powerful.

Moral Imagination

It may be that the deficiency of our thinking about unborn human life stems from a certain failure of imagination. Imagination, as distinct from fantasy, requires us to conceptualise from another's perspective, to stand in their shoes and to feel their situation. Because we rarely see unborn life, and because almost all of us cannot claim to remember embryonic existence, it is easy for our moral convictions to be dictated by purely *memorised* existence. So often we live - perhaps unconsciously - by the dictum: what we cannot remember; we never were. To be a full human being, however, involves us in the multifaceted business of holding together disparate truths; different stages as well as memories of life. To hold that embryonic life has no clear relationship to ourselves, indeed to posit that it is not part of ourselves, is a symptom of fragmented and confused existence. Imagination is central to being fully human because, as Rachel Trickett observes, it 'holds in the mind the completeness of a complex truth with all its many facets'.[38] Perhaps it is here that the poet can help us with a fuller picture of what being human is all about. Louis Macneice, in his remarkable poem *Prayer Before Birth*, articulates the radical vulnerability involved in embryonic existence:

> I am not yet born; forgive me
> For the sins that in me the world shall commit, my words
> when they speak me, my thoughts when they think me,
> my treason engendered by traitors beyond me,
> my life when they murder by means of my
> hands, my death when they live me...
>
> I am not yet born; O hear me,
> Let not the man who is beast or who thinks he is God come
> near me.

Writing before 1940, Macneice could scarcely have envisaged the modern developments in experimental science that would so radically exploit the vulnerability of the human embryo. And yet there is more than a faint hint of pre-cognition in this final, passionate stanza:

> I am not yet born; O fill me
> With strength against those who would freeze my
> humanity, would dragoon me into a lethal automaton,
> would make me a cog in a machine, a thing with
> one face, a thing, and against all those
> who would dissipate my entirety, would
> blow me like thistledown hither and
> thither or hither and thither
> like water held in the
> hands would spill me
> Let them not make me a stone and let them not spill me.
> Otherwise kill me.[39]

Those who criticise this poetical imagination, should contemplate what the world would be like without any sense of solidarity with, and respect for, our human origins. To be imaginatively in touch with all the kinds and stages of human existence, however apparently removed from us, might be one capacity that saves each one of us from becoming the 'things' of which Macneice speaks.

Otiose Arguments

It will be noticed that we have not made use of a number of arguments that are commonly brought against those who support experimentation on embryos. We have not for example brought into play the idea of the 'innocency' of unborn life. Such a notion may conceivably be coherent when applied to unborn humans (though surely less so when used in relationship to adult humans) but does not seem in either case to be morally relevant. It rests essentially upon *human* notions of guilt and innocence which seem to be impossible to reconcile with the teaching of Jesus which emphasises the love of God equally for sinners as for the righteous. Indeed the very term 'righteous' has a certain ironical flavour as used in context by some of the New Testament writers.[40]

Neither have we used the argument drawn from certain qualitative characteristics, such as consciousness and sentiency, which embryos may or may not be said to possess. It may be that embryos are sentient in ways in which we do not at present appreciate or it may be said that they are not. It may be said that embryos are more consciously existing subjects even at this early stage of life than we appreciate. It may be or it may not be. It may well be that outside the human community the question about the kind and quality of life is important in some way and one of us has sought to give some account of them elsewhere.[41] But we have already shown how such procedures seem to be largely irrelevant when it comes to deciding what kind of status a human being should have. When we are faced with second-order situations of conflict, we may well have to make some kind of judgement, albeit temporary and largely arbitrary, about the quality of one human life in contrast with another. But these are surely distinctions *in extremis*, and should not determine from the outset what value a member of the human community should have as a matter of principle or precept. The whole attempt to delineate qualities or characteristics which some human subjects may be said to possess and others do not invariably leads, and has lead historically, to the disparagement of some humans as inferior, second class or substandard. If we take our stand on the life and example of Jesus Christ we shall oppose all man-made attempts to determine the worth of some humans against others from a purely qualitative point of view. The central theological point to be remembered here, simple as it is profound, is that God's mysterious love alone qualifies every human being as a subject of irreducible value.

Conclusion

In sum, our argument in this chapter has been as follows: that the Gospel emphasis upon the prior moral claim of the weak, exemplified by Jesus' own identification with the poor, the vulnerable and the captive, needs to be taken a great deal more seriously by Christian theologians and moralists than hitherto. When related to modern thinking about the status of the embryo and especially its use in scientific research, the arguments presented in favour of this practice do not stand much theological scrutiny. In short the 'leastness' of the embryo and its relative weakness in the human community, far from being an argument for its exploitation, may be the one consideration that should make adult humans draw back from the exercise of power.

4

SUBMISSION: THE LIMITS TO EMBRYONIC RESEARCH

Introduction

1. The Department of Health and Social Security in its document Cm 46 has invited responses with a view to wide consultation prior to the introduction of legislation relating to the recommendations of the Warnock Committee on embryonic research and surrogacy. The principal concern of our submission is directed to the problem of **Research involving human embryos** as outlined in paragraghs 45-60 of Cm 46. Paragraph 59 of Cm 46 suggests that Parliament will be offered a Bill containing two alternative and apparently exclusive clauses. The first optional clause would allow experimentation, under the aegis of a licensing authority, on human embryos up to a period of fourteen days after fertilisation, the second optional clause would 'prohibit all research except that which was intended to be of benefit to the individual embryo.'

2. In this submission it is argued that the two options offered in the proposed Bill are not mutually exclusive, that both options permit research on embryos, and that both options rest on a hidden and putative distinction between *therapeutic* and *non-therapeutic research*. Research directed to the well-being of the individual embryo could be interpreted as sanctioning a more general research programme within which it might be argued benefit to the individual embryo was obtained. Alternatively it might be argued that a *general* research

programme was necessary to meet the objectives, intentions and aims of the second option. In order to avoid these potential difficulties, we propose that the aims and objectives of the second optional clause to be put to Parliament be modified under the terms of paragraph 60 of Cm 46. Paragraph 60 of Cm 46 allows for 'Any other variant' on the two options offered in Paragraph 59 to 'be put forward' during the passage of the Bill. Paragraph 3 of this submission summarises one such variant. The balance of this submission presents arguments for that variant.

3. In this submission it is proposed that any and all embryonic research should be completely prohibited even if that research falls under either of the two options of paragraph 59 of Cm 46. It is argued that in the area of embryonic research there is no valid distinction between *therapeutic* and *non-therapeutic research*. It is agreed, however, that there is a valid distinction between therapeutic *intervention* and therapeutic *research* and it is suggested that a third 'variant' in accordance with the option of paragraph 60 of Cm 46 be added to the proposed Bill which would allow for limited instances of therapeutic *intervention* where that intervention is solely necessary for the welfare of the individual zygote. This proposed third 'variant' is different from the options of paragraph 59 of Cm 46 in that it differentiates between '...all *research* except that which was intended to be of benefit to the individual embryo' and *'therapeutic intervention* which is intended to be of benefit to the individual embryo.' The importance of this distinction, if implemented, is that it forestalls some of the difficulties outlined in paragraph 2 of this submission and which are inherent in the second optional clause as expressed in paragraph 59 of Cm 46.

4. The arguments of this submission do not address the issue of surrogacy. If the recommendations made here are adopted the issue of surrogacy will arise only in the most exceptional of cases and the only grounds for the institutionalisation of arrangements for surrogacy would be for the therapeutic welfare of the zygote. If

the optional clause suggested in paragraph 3 of this submission were adopted then it would automatically follow that any non-therapeutic surrogacy arrangements would be prohibited.

5. It is a consequence of the arguments presented here that legislation should be introduced to prevent the use of 'spare' embryos or zygotes for research directed either at the 'general interest of science' or for some putative and ill defined 'general benefit'. The current state of I.V.F. is such that it is a not infrequent consequence of such programmes that so-called 'spare' zygotes are produced. The present legal position accords no statutory restriction on embryonic research. The current voluntary controls, while accepting the general guidelines of the Warnock Committee suffer from the disadvantage of a) lacking statutory force, and b) not being universally applied. In this submission it will be argued that zygotes do have a moral status, should be entitled to the protection of law, and that a specific section of legislation aimed at prohibiting harm to zygotes be introduced. It is proposed that a specific criminal offence of '**zygocide**' be introduced carrying penalties similar to those to be found in the **Infertility Medical Procedures Act (Victoria) 1984.** That Act allows for penalties of up to four years imprisonment for actions designed to interfere with the normal development of potential human life.

6. Further specific recommendations supportive of the proposed third 'variant' allowed under the terms of paragraph 60 of Cm 46 are presented. Each of these recommendations is supported both by general and specific arguments. Those arguments are presented principally in the kinds of terms set out in Cm 46 and in the terms of the Warnock Commission. However, acceptance of those terms for present purposes does not imply anything other than the reluctant and pragmatic recognition that those terms are dictated largely by the language and concepts of the present debate. That language itself is based on the interests of scientific research rather than on the well-being and the intrinsic value of the embryo/zygote.

7. The conceptual and linguistic background to Cm 46 is restricted by the factors outlined in paragraph 6 of this submission and this paper makes not only specific recommendations but also points in paragraph 33 to the restricted way in which the terms of the debate on the issue of the status of the embryo have been set and points to the conceptual poverty associated with the meaningfulness of the genetic origins of human life. While the terms of the debate as set by Cm 46 and while the arguments presented here are developed largely in those terms, the presentation of those arguments does not imply either part or wholesale acceptance of the conceptual poverty of Cm 46 in respect of the issues presented either in the consultative document or any of its precursors.

The Creation of Embryos

8. The initial purpose of the formation of embryos *in vitro* was to assist in overcoming certain forms of sterility. First pregnancies were achieved in the early 1970's. The first live birth was in 1978. The success rates during those first few years were zero. A U.S. study reported that the success rates even now are only slightly greater than those obtained from a random sample of couples classed as infertile on the same grounds as those classed as infertile but entered into an I.V.F. programme.[1]

   I.V.F. clinics repeatedly tend to report success rates higher than this. Cm 46 suggests a success rate of the order of fifteen per cent but this is a wildly optimistic figure and is strongly disputed by several authorities (see paragraphs 11-14 below). The reason for this discrepancy arises partly as a result of classification problems and partly as a result of some clinics counting experimental procedures which do not lead to live non-deformed birth as complete success. In assessing the success rates of I.V.F. techniques mere experimental success should be discounted and common criteria of measurement established.

9. A confusion of criteria of the success of I.V.F. arises partly as a result of differing causes of infertility and partly as a result of differing techniques used to overcome infertility. Infertility affects somewhere between 10 and 20 per cent of couples in the peak child producing years. The cause of infertility is probably divided equally between men and women. Initially, therefore, I.V.F. was appropriate only when the women is infertile and even then only when the cause of the infertility is due to definite and limited factors. Female infertility is principally caused by previous sterilisation, abortion, pelvic inflammatory disease, cervical mucous problems, defects in ovulation and blocked fallopian tubes. Male infertility may, in principle, be dealt with by the micro-injection of sperm into the ovum. Nevertheless of infertile couples very few meet the criteria necessary

for entry into an I.V.F. programme. Exclusion may be advised on a wide variety of clinical, psychological or social grounds.

10. Several different techniques of I.V.F. are available most of which require the extraction of ovum from the women. This procedure generally requires the prescription of a drug to overstimulate ovarian production. Such drugs frequently lead to severe depression and a high number of women do leave the programme as a direct consequence of the depressive effects of ovarian hyperstimulants. The next stage in the procedure is the extraction of a number of ova by laparoscopy: a surgically invasive procedure designed to collect five or six ova. The ova are then placed in a culture and incubated for about twelve hours before a sample of as much as fifty thousand sperm are added to each ovum. At some point after this stage a conceptus is formed which, if normal, has all the genetic information required for a future full, complete and individual life. Further incubation then takes place. After 24 hours cell division has clearly developed and the embryo is transferred into the womb by a further, though relatively minor, invasive procedure. An alternative procedure Gamete Intra Fallopian Transfer is similarly invasive in requiring laparoscopy. After that point the technique has some variations in application but, in general, one ovum and a sample of sperm are placed in the end of each fallopian tube. The procedure requires a general anaesthetic.

11. Ovarian hyperstimulation is required in I.V.F. in order to producemore ova than are strictly required to bring about one pregnancy. The failure rate of I.V.F. is sufficiently high that if one ova were obtained and pregnancy did not result then a further invasive laparoscopy would be required. Consequently the normal I.V.F. procedure presents a dilemma. Either all satisfactorily fertilised ovum are placed in the womb in the hope that one or more will develop to term or, bearing in mind the risk of multiple pregnancy should all six come to term, some fertilised ovum are not placed in the womb but are either destroyed or frozen for further use. In practice the success

rate is so low that it is unlikely that all six fertilised ovum will develop in the womb. But to rely on that calculation creates a further potential problem. Should all six ovum take then the mother's health is placed at risk but if it is calculated that this outcome is unlikely, due to the failure rate, then such calculation presupposes that the moral status of the fertilised embryos is of little or no consequence. In the unlikely event of all six embryos 'taking' the mother's health is placed at risk to an extent which some practitioners regard as being sufficiently severe to justify selective termination of some of the foetuses. This procedure while probably legal under the terms of the 1967 Abortion Act is condemned by the current Voluntary Licensing Authority. The combination of the practice of multiple implantation and selective termination against the advice of the current V.L.A. indicates a failure of voluntary arrangements and the need for clear and unequivocal statutory guidelines backed by unambiguous penalties for breach of the guidelines.

12. It is also clear that whether all six fertilised ovum are placed in the womb or whether the 'spare' embryos are destroyed, the I.V.F. procedure is based on an indifference to the moral status of the embryo. An alternative approach to destroying the unused embryos is to freeze and store them. Embryo freezing was first developed at Monash University. About 50 percent of embryos survive freezing and subsequent thawing. About 2 per cent of all embryos frozen, thawed and implanted result in live births.[2]

    In assessing the import of this figure it should be noted that the figure is arrived at from successful laparoscopy and fertilisation rather then from entry to an I.V.F. programme and should, therefore, be judged in that light. If the figures included entry to an I.V.F. programme to live non-malformed birth (see paragraphs 8 and 9 above and paragraphs 13 and 14 below) then the true figures may be even lower than given here.

13. As noted in paragraph 8, measurements of success vary. Discounting experimental criteria estimates also vary also by virtue of the use of differing criteria. The clearest category would be the number of live, non-malformed births produced from acceptance into an I.V.F. programme. However, it is a common practice to base success rates on the number of pregnancies per laparoscopy. This latter figure thus excludes the number of women who leave the programme because of depressive problems resulting from ovarian hyperstimulants and excludes those numbers of women whose I.V.F. treatment results in miscarriage or deformed birth. It is too early to determine the long term well-being or otherwise of children born as a result of I.V.F. and too early to determine the long term effects of freezing the zygote. It is not impossible that long term harm will result to those born as a result of the programme and to that extent *the entire I.V.F. programme is experimental* and will remain so for the lifetime of the entire generation of those persons born as a result of I.V.F. Indeed there are some reservations that the experimental time span of the programme will actually be longer than one generation as any future offspring of I.V.F. children may themselves suffer from long term difficulties. Leaving these problems aside, however, it is clear that counting success as being merely the rate between laparoscopy and pregnancy biases the figures towards success and goes some way to explaining the claims that the success rate is as high as 15 per cent. But even that criteria of success understates the real failure rate for it fails to take into account the number of fertilised embryos produced which having the potential capacity for life are not allowed that potential and which are counted as 'spare' embryos or which are destroyed.

14. Taking 'success' as being based on the first criteria: namely from entry to the programme to a successful and normal live birth the success rate is maximally 2 per cent. If the embryo has been frozen then using the same criteria the rate is significantly lower. A success rate of the order of 2 per cent is so low that it is not surprising that the comparison with a control group referred to in paragraph 8 of

this submission could show no statistically significant difference between the two groups at any acceptable level of confidence. If 'spare' embryos, embryos which are destroyed, embryos which fail to implant, terminations and malformed births are taken into account in calculating the effect of current I.V.F. rates then it is not the *success* rate of I.V.F. which should be examined but the *failure* rate. That failure rate is statistically significant.

Experimentation

15. The issue of embryo research arises principally from the possibility that I.V.F. programmes generate more embryos than are required for dealing with the problems of fertility. However, paragraph 55 of Cm 46 raises the possibility of the specific donation of gametes for the production of embryos for research. Paragraph 55 also draws a distinction between embryos specifically created for research and research on so called 'spare' embryos. Some members of the Warnock Committee favoured permitting research on 'spare' embryos. It is understandable that some members of the Warnock Committee should feel that the production of embryos purely for the purpose of research was more difficult to justify than permitting research on so called 'spare embryos', however, we must insist that the distinction between embryos created for research and research on 'spare' embryos is unsound. If it is ethically unsound to experiment on embryos then it is unsound wherever or whatever the source of the embryo. If the embryo has some kind of moral status, however that might be understood, then it has that status intrinsically regardless of the manner by which it was brought into being and regardless of its source.

16. The distinctions between the two optional clauses offered in paragraph 59 of Cm 46 - their implications and potential difficulties referred to and outlined in paragraph 2 of this submission - reflect a confusion with respect to research protocols. It is clear that part of paragraphs 55-59 of Cm 46 rests on the distinctions and protocols expressed in the Declaration of Helsinki adopted by the 18th. World Medical Assembly at Helsinki in 1964 and revised at the Second Declaration of Helsinki adopted in Tokyo at the 29th World Medical Assembly, Tokyo, Japan, 1975. All following references to the Declaration of Helsinki refer to the 1975 revised version.

17. The Declaration of Helsinki provides guidelines for biomedical research involving human subjects and accepts in its **Introduction** that 'Medical progress is based on research which ultimately must rest in part on experimentation involving human subjects.' The declaration draws a distinction between '...research in which the aim is essentially diagnostic or therapeutic for a patient, and medical research, the essential object of which is purely scientific and without direct diagnostic or therapeutic value to the person involved in the research.' By accepting research as a common element in both of the optional clauses offered in paragraph 59 of Cm 46 that document implicitly relies on the distinction between therapeutic research and non-therapeutic research. The apparently mutually exclusive options expressed in paragraph 59 of Cm 46 appear to rely on this distinction with the second option implicitly accepting the notion of research which is designed to be therapeutic as being sufficient to safeguard the intentions of the framers of the **Unborn Children (Protection) Bill.** As stated in paragraph 2 of this submission, we doubt whether the second option, as currently framed would meet those aims and intentions. We also feel, in the light of experience in Australia, that the second optional clause, as expressed in paragraph 59 of Cm 46 would be open to a wider interpretation by any statutory licensing authority than was intended by the sponsors of the clause. We also feel, again in the light of recent Australian experience, that the wording of the second optional clause leaves itself open to legal challenge the effect of which might be to expand the original intentions of the sponsors beyond that which they desired. We also feel that any legislation supporting any restriction on research or any legislation prohibiting research should not allow any statutory authority, whether it be a licensing authority or the relevant Secretary of State, any discretion about what does or does not count as the beginning of life. This particular problem will be explored in paragraphs 29-37 below, but the recommendation here is made in the light of the recent decision of the Solicitor General of Victoria to advise against the promulgation of that section of the Victorian **Infertility (Medical Procedures) Act 1984** which dealt with the

origins of human life. The effect of the Solicitor General's actions has been to a) thwart the intentions of the Victorian Parliament, and b) produce a deadlock in the licensing authority as to what research may or may not be permitted. These kinds of problems are clear indications of the difficulties that can arise if parliamentary indications are not precise, clear and unambiguous. At least some of these dangers and ambiguities can be removed or reduced by careful attention, first, to well established practices and medical protocols and second, by learning from the experience of other legislatures in this area.

18. The distinction between therapeutic research and non-therapeutic research overlooks an important distinction made in the Second Declaration of Helsinki. The second declaration clarifies, refines and qualifies the distinction between therapeutic and non-therapeutic research. Section two of the Second Declaration of Helsinki expands on the distinction between therapeutic and non-therapeutic research in favour of a distinction made in section III of the Declaration of Helsinki between *MEDICAL RESEARCH COMBINED WITH CLINICAL CARE* : referred to as 'Clinical Research' where the principal object is the well-being of the patient and *NON-THERAPEUTIC BIOMEDICAL RESEARCH INVOLVING HUMAN SUBJECTS* : referred to as 'Non-clinical biomedical research'.

19. The Declaration of Helsinki makes it clear that such research is subject to certain restrictions: first the health of the person on whom the research is to be carried out, second, that the *subjects* should be volunteers, a notion that implies some form of informed consent, and finally that, notwithstanding the benefits to research 'the interests of science and society should never take precedence over considerations related to the well-being of the subject.'

20. By relying on a distinction between therapeutic and non-therapeutic research, Cm 46 implicitly accepts part of the Helsinki protocol. However, Cm 46 ignores the qualifying clauses in that declaration which make it clear that the crucial distinction is between Clinical research combined with clinical care and Non-clinical biomedical research. In both cases the well-being of the subject is paramount and in both cases some notion of consent on the part of the subject is either implied or made explicit. Clearly no embryo, pre-embryo or zygote is in a position to consent to any form of research. Equally clearly, if such consent could, counterfactually, be obtained it is unlikely that such consent would exclude clinical care. Whether consent can or cannot be obtained the Declaration of Helsinki makes it clear that the interests of the subject must be paramount.

21. Insofar as those who draw a distinction between therapeutic research and non-therapeutic research rest their ethical case on the Declaration of Helsinki, then whether they consider the exercise that they plan to undertake as clinical or non-clinical the well-being of the subject or patient is paramount. If the patient is the embryo then it is the well-being of the embryo that must prevail. In that case any destructive non-clinical research would appear to be unethical. Such research is neither in the immediate interests of the mother or of the embryo and its only justification would be some putative long term benefit to 'the interests of science or of society' both of which are aims that are condemned in the Third Section of the Declaration of Helsinki.

22. Two principal objections might be raised against the line of reasoning leading to the conclusion of paragraph 21 of this submission. First, it might be objected that the embryo is not a subject deserving of moral consideration, or second that insofar as it is deserving of moral consideration such consideration applies only in the case of those embryos formed in good faith with the intention of bringing them, if possible, to a full human life. Insofar as the first objection is concerned the exact moral status of the embryo will be considered

later, but in the immediate context of this section it seems clear that once a doctor has assumed responsibility for a patient in an I.V.F. programme that same doctor has accepted as his patient not only the mother - but also any embryo that he causes to be brought into being.

23. It may well be that the responsibility of the doctor to the embryo is greater than his or her responsibility to the mother. Infertility is a social problem with medical implications; it is distressing to those concerned but infertility is not of itself directly life threatening. The actions taken with respect to the embryo, however, are directly life threatening. Decisions taken with respect to a particular embryo may determine whether a unique individual obtains a full chance of human life or not. It may be that the real clinical responsibility is less to the potential mother and more to the embryo. In the former case, life may be distressing and burdensome. In the latter case, life may, by virtue of a casual decision as to which embryo to implant and which embryo on which to undertake research, never reach the point at which it is permitted the opportunities of joy, burden and distress: all features of a normal human life. Often our duties to the weaker are greater than our duties to the stronger and our duties to the weaker often take the form of stewardship or guardianship. We suggest that we do owe duties to embryos and that those duties are best expressed through the notion of steward or guardian. We further suggest that it is the doctor or clinician who is in the best position to act as an agent of society in meeting those duties. If this suggestion is accepted then notwithstanding any duty that a doctor may have to the potential mother that doctor will also have duty of care to the embryo. Such an ethical stance would eliminate any action not designed to enhance the well-being of the embryo.

24. Avoiding the implications of paragraph 23 of this submission requires either denying that the embryo is an entity worthy of moral consideration or allowing it some kind of status only if it was to be implanted. However, any moral status that the embryo has would be

denied if it was held that the embryo was 'spare' or if it were argued that embryos specifically created for research have no status independent of the purpose for which they were created: namely the aims and interests of the scientist who fused the natural gametes of the donor. All of these arguments are implicitly to be found in paragraph 55 of Cm 46. All of these arguments rest on some misconceptions.

25. The principle function and aims of I.V.F. programmes is to deal with infertility. Implicit in, and inseparable from, that aim is the production of a new and distinctive human life. If that new and distinctive human life is not brought into being then the problem of infertility has not been dealt with. In this submission it is taken as axiomatic that all human life has some moral status. It follows that a physical precondition of that moral status is birth and conception. The conceptus is the earliest *physical* precondition of human moral status. Whatever the exact moral status of the conceptus might be it certainly has that minimal standing.

26. An unmodified distinction between therapeutic research and non-therapeutic research is dubious in that it alters the exact terms of the Declaration of Helsinki. It is also scientifically dubious. It is far from clear that any therapeutic research on a zygote that could be undertaken at the moment would be of direct clinical value to the particular zygote on which the research was undertaken. Such research is likely to be so invasive that it would destroy or threaten the well-being of the zygote on which the research was being undertaken. If that destruction was the likely outcome of such research then that research could hardly be said to be therapeutic. The only possible non-destructive exception on the scientific horizon at the moment is the taking of a cell from a zygote at the early stages of cell division with a view to testing for chromosomatic abnormalities. It has been argued that such an action would not interfere with the normal development of the zygote.

27. The extraction of a cell from a zygote and the testing for chromosomatic or genetic defects does, itself, raise serious moral problems. At this point in time, and at any future conceivable point in time, it is unclear whether, even if genetic defects were found in the zygote that they could be corrected. If genetic defects were observed then the options are implantation of a genetically defective zygote or the destruction of that zygote. It is already standard practice not to implant zygotes where gross abnormalities can be observed after initial cell division. Presumably testing for chromosomatic abnormalities is proposed as an extension of current practice. The objections raised here to this extension of current practice is that it conceals a Eugenic programme.

28. Cm 46 succeeds in hiding an important issue. The practices referred to in paragraph 27 of this document are implicitly or explicitly eugenic in their effects. Paragraphs 55 and 59 of Cm 46 implicitly support options which in practice are almost certain to lead to a Eugenic programme. Paragraph 49 of Cm 46 refers to 'embryo biopsy' and in a footnote to that paragraph claims that this would, 'give the possibility in some instances of rejecting defective embryos in favour of healthy ones...'. This practice if implemented begs a number of questions of principle including what is or is not to be counted as healthy and who is or is not to decide the criteria by which any particular embryo is or is not to be counted as healthy enough to be brought to post-natal life. Paragraph 49 of Cm 46 clearly rests on some notion which encompasses a view about the 'quality of life' as opposed to some notion of the 'sanctity of life' but fails to outline any means by which the principle of the 'quality of life' is to be implemented or to state who is to determine whether a life has sufficient 'quality' to be brought into being. Such a view is clearly eugenic for it implies some view about what health or other characteristics future generations will have and would seek to achieve this aim by the selective destruction of embryos deemed unfit for life. Whatever the moral arguments about such a eugenic programme might be it is certainly improper to embark upon such a programme

explicitly or implicitly without full consultation with all sectors of society. It is certainly improper to offer Members of Parliament a Bill which contains two optional clauses both of which include, yet hide, a Eugenic programme. The Bill proposed in paragraph 59 of Cm 46 does just that and in doing so it not only hides the important Eugenic element of the Bill, it also over-rides that part of the Second Declaration of Helsinki, quoted in paragraph 19 of this paper that, 'the interests of science and society should never take precedence over considerations related to the well-being of the subject.' Cm 46 reflects contempt for an internationally endorsed protocol.

The Moral Status of the Embryo

29. There has been considerable debate about the precise moral standing of the embryo. If the embryo, zygote or conceptus has no moral standing then it has been argued that any and all experimentation on an embryo would be permitted. The standing of the embryo would be that of a mere object of scientific interest. As such it could be treated in the same way as any other object of scientific interest. Nevertheless even those who advocate research on human embryos draw the line at some point. Beyond that point, it is argued, research should be prohibited. The exact point at which the line should be drawn is disputed but the common acceptance that there is a 'marker event' or point beyond which research should be prohibited indicates a common acceptance that at some point in its development the embryo does have some moral standing and is due some moral respect. A question worthy of exploration hinges on whether this common ground is indicative of quantitative differences in the development of the embryo and its standing or whether this common ground points to qualitative differences in the development of the embryo and its moral standing. Some examples will clarify these distinctions.

30. It has been argued, notably by Professor Peter Singer of Monash University, that experimentation on embryos would be morally permissible up to a period of six weeks after conception. The rationale for this line of thinking is that as the nervous system of the embryo has not developed until that point it could not feel pain. Singer accepts that experimentation beyond that point would be morally wrong as the embryo would suffer distress of a particular type. The criteria that Singer is using are qualitative; that is to say that there is some particular and specific point in the development of the embryo at which the embryo comes to have a moral standing which hitherto it did not have. Singer's argument is based on clear utilitarian criteria and we would reject it on those grounds alone. However, we also find it unsatisfactory even in its own terms. The

mere absence of pain, or of a pain mechanism, seems a poor criteria on which to assess moral standing. It cannot be assumed that in the absence of physical pain as we understand it that some other form of trauma cannot be experienced by a six week embryo. Nor are we satisfied that there is some distinct point in time after conception at which that which has been a non-moral object becomes a moral subject. We reject, therefore, the idea of a distinct and qualitative alteration in the moral status of the developing embryo.

31. Paragraph 55 of Cm 46 suggests a 14 day time limit on embryo research. Paragraph 59 offers, as one of the optional clauses in the proposed Bill, research up to a period of 14 days after fertilisation. In reaching this period of time the Warnock Commission was unable to determine any particular point in time at which it could be said that human life began. The 14 day period is taken to be the point in the natural cycle of pregnancy at which the fertilised ovum will implant. In the normal course of events such implantation often fails. Further, some forms of contraception are effective by virtue of preventing implantation. By extension - both from normal risk and from standardly accepted contraceptive practice - it seemed to some that it was only quantitatively different to allow research up until the 14 day period. It is already accepted as a fact of nature and as a standard contraceptive practice that a 14 day embryo/zygote is at natural risk or may be destroyed by some contraceptive means. Hence it seemed that what is naturally at risk may be used for scientific purposes without moral compromise. On this view there is no qualitative difference between the proposed research activities and the course of nature. We reject this view and its implications. The matter of contraceptive practice is outside our purview but insofar as that argument is imported into the issue of research on embryos it rests on the mistake of taking one practice with a particular and specific intent and utilising it for another practice with a different intent. Clearly that kind of argument cannot be properly used to determine the moral standing of the embryo. Insofar as the natural risk in the first 14 days is concerned similar objections apply. Human life is full

of natural risks but that a natural risk exists scarcely excuses turning it into a deliberately manufactured risk.

32. Some recent arguments in Australia have turned on the point of *syngamy*, the stage at which the nuclei of the zygote fuse: a stage reached approximately 20-22 hours after fertilisation. The **Infertility Medical Procedures Act (Victoria) 1984** which prohibits research on embryos has recently come under legal challenge on the grounds that an embryo is not formed until syngamy: hence research up until a period of 22 hours should be permitted under the terms of the Act. This challenge is, in part, the result of a drafting error in the Bill which took the meaning of the term 'embryo' to be unambiguous. 'Syngamy', like the 14 day period or even the six week period, is part of an ongoing search for a marker event at which life can be said to begin. This in turn forms part of a wider case for permitting some experimentation on human embryos. In the case of 'syngamy' this case is being made even in a context when it was intended that any procedure carried out on an embryo which reduced the prospects of pregnancy was to be expressly forbidden by Statute.

33. We do accept that there is a 'marker event' at which human life can be said to begin but we reject the six week period, the 14 day period and 'syngamy'. All of these attempts to determine a 'marker event' rest on some kind of scientific claims about what does or does not count as the origin of human life or what does or does not count as 'trauma'. Such forms of discussion show how the issues involved have been couched in scientific terms and in following those terms alone Cm 46 has the kind of conceptual poverty referred to in paragraph 6 and 7 of this submission. It is not clear to us that the absence of pain would exclude trauma of some other kind, nor is it clear to us that some kind of trauma could not be experienced at even very early stages of development. While we cannot make any positive claim that an early embryo could not experience trauma of some kind, we can find no evidence to exclude that possibility and feel that the onus is on those who would deny such a possibility to prove their claim

beyond any doubt. We do not wish, here, to enter into traditional arguments about ensoulment but we would wish to ask *if* ensoulment did take place at the moment of conception then what would be the consequences of experimentation and what would be the consequences of the long term freezing of embryos? In the latter case the consequence would be something akin to a humanly endowed period of purgatory. The thought might be far-fetched but we would wish to know whether it is so far-fetched that any one of us living now would wish to have been permanently placed in that kind of situation. We would also wish to know whether the scientific discourse within which these issues are debated is so firmly grounded that there can be no doubt whatsoever that possibilities couched in other forms of discourse have no basis.

34. We propose that the 'marker event' at which human life can properly be said to begin is that point of fertilisation when the genetic material of the sperm is released into the ovum. Put another way life begins when the individuality of the gametes is lost in favour of a new and distinct entity: a single cell having the capacity for pairing. 'Syngamy' occurs at the point when chromosomal pairing occurs. But even prior to that the ovum and the sperm had united into a single cell having the capacity for pairing. Any 'marker event' beyond this is fraught with difficulty being merely an attempt to use extrinsic criteria for a purpose to which they are not suited. Even the Warnock Committee conceded that '...there is no particular part of the developmental process that is more important than another; all are part of a continuous process.' This implies acceptance of a quantitative view of human development yet Warnock found a qualitative 'marker event' at 14 days. The stated reason for this was that '...we agreed that this was an area in which some precise decision must be taken in order to allay public anxiety.' [3]

35. Any 'marker event' to be satisfactory must show some qualitative difference between the state of affairs before the event and the state of affairs following the event. No scientific, philosophical or

theological evidence has clearly shown anything other than a developmental process following fertilisation as defined in paragraph 33. of this submission. No government committee or legal challenge has ever demonstrated that any 'marker event' other than fertilisation is based on anything other than extrinsic criteria. We are, therefore, persuaded by the arguments of The Australian ***Senate*** *Select Committee On The Human Embryo Experimentation Bill 1985*, chaired by Senator Tate, that the embryo should be 'regarded as genetically new human life organised as a distinct entity oriented towards further development.'[4]

36. Tate further regards the embryo from the moment of fertilisation as deserving of respect due to 'deference of the embryo's human and social future'[5] and while denying that the embryo is a person asserts that it is a 'human subject'. We accept that the embryo is not an actual person in the standard philosophical sense of having the actual capacities of willing, desiring, thinking, forming projects, etc. Tate fails to explain why an embryo is a human subject but we accept that there is no necessary connection in a moral sense between the notions of 'person' and the notion of 'subject'. It is quite possible for an entity to be a moral subject without being a person in the strict philosophical sense. A moral subject is deserving of respect and of medical treatment in accordance with the Declaration of Helsinki. Insofar as that subject is unable to provide consent as enunciated in accordance with that Declaration then the provisions of that Declaration relating to the care of those unable to consent should be observed.

37. In concluding this section, we observe that there is no distinct 'marker event' beyond carefully defined fertilisation which would cause us to regard the entity brought into being at that point as anything other than a Genetically Organised Distinct Subject [which is] Emergent [and] Newly Developing (GODSEND).

Recommendations[6]

38. 1. That a distinction be drawn between therapeutic *research* and therapeutic *intervention* (paragraph 2 and 3).

2. The second option of paragraph 59 of Cm 46 be modified to read '...to prohibit all research on embryos but to permit limited intervention where that intervention is solely for the well-being of the individual embryo' (paragraphs 2 and 3).

3. That surrogacy arrangements be permitted only where required to meet the needs of recommendation 38.2 (paragraph 4).

4. That statutory controls be established to ensure that any I.V.F. programme is properly supervised and licensed; that a statutory licensing authority be established, that such authority be required to report to the Secretary of State and to Parliament in accord with the recommendations made below and that any breach of the terms of any such license be made a criminal offence (paragraph 5).

5. That no I.V.F. procedure be permitted except by a properly competent and duly licensed authority (paragraph 5).

6. That no licence be granted for any purpose other than ensuring the well-being of the individual embryo and that no license be granted for any general research programme (paragraphs 1-6).

7. That common criteria of measurement of the success of I.V.F. programmes be established. That such criteria be taken as encompassing the range from requests to enter an I.V.F. programme to successful non-malformed live births (paragraphs 8, and 11-14).

8. That the statutory licensing authority be required to collect accurate statistics in order to assess the real efficacy of I.V.F. programmes and that the statutory licensing authority be required to report annually to the Secretary of State and to Parliament (paragraphs 8, and 11-14).

9. That the statutory licensing authority include in its statistical collation and annual report the depressive effects of ovarian hyperstimulation (paragraph 10)

10. That the statutory licensing authority require the prohibition or termination of any procedure which places the health of the mother at risk and that any procedure which is likely to lead to multiple pregnancy and selective termination of implanted embryos be prohibited (paragraph 11).

11. That the freezing of embryos be prohibited except where there is no alternative to that procedure to safeguard the potential well-being of the individual embryo. That consideration be given to the development of techniques for the freezing of individual gametes rather than the fertilised embryo (paragraphs 12 and 33).

12. That the entire I.V.F. programme be regarded as experimental and that the programme be regarded as experimental for at least three generations (paragraph 13).

13. That the notion of spare embryos be regarded as merely a product of the failure of I.V.F. procedures, that the notion of spare embryos is morally degrading, that research on so-called spare embryos be prohibited and that due respect is accorded to all embryos (paragraphs 13, 29, and 36).

14. That no embryos be created specifically for the purpose of research and that no donor gametes be fertilised for the purpose of research (paragraphs 15 and 24).

15. That the beginning of life be defined for legislative purposes as occurring at the moment of conception and that such definition be included in any Act of Parliament (paragraphs 17, and 34).

16. That for the purposes of legislation and control the embryo, from the moment of conception, be regarded as a moral subject and that the ethical protocols of the Second Declaration of Helsinki be regarded as applying fully to embryos (paragraghs 19-20 and 36).

17. That the interests of 'science or of society' should never take precedence over the interests of the individual embryo (paragraph 21).

18. That any clinician involved in any I.V.F. programme regards not only the mother but the embryo as his or her patient and that any such clinician owes a duty of care to the embryo (paragraph 22).

19. That infertility be regarded as a social problem with medical sequlae and not as a medical problem with social sequlae. The statutory licensing authority should be empowered to inquire into, make regulations and enforce full and adequate counselling to any applicant to an I.V.F. programme. The statutory licensing authority should ensure that counselling is complete, that the risks are explained fully, that consent is freely obtained, that such consent be informed and that every possible alternative avenue to what is principally a social problem be explored before admission to an I.V.F. programme is approved. The licensing authority should be required to gather and collate sociological data with respect to the social aspects of infertility and to report on the results of such investigations (paragraph 23).

20. That testing for chromosomatic abnormalities, selective rejection of embryos and selective termination is negatively and destructively eugenic in its effects. If such practices were carried out on developed human beings they would be roundly condemned. The eugenic

element contained in Cm 46 should be expanded, clarified and put to Parliament. It is recommended that Parliament use its powers to require the proposed statutory licensing authority to prohibit any procedure that is designed to be, or is likely to be, eugenic in its effects (paragraphs 27-28).

21. That the only sound and satisfactory 'marker event' which designates the beginning of human life is fertilisation which we define as the point at which the genetic material of the sperm is released into the ovum. We recommend that this definition be incorporated into the appropriate legislation (paragraph 34). We have examined other alternatives and found them unsatisfactory (paragraphs 29-32).

22. That the possibility of a form of trauma to an early embryo which is not accountable for in the terms of scientific discourse cannot *a-priori* be eliminated. The statutory licensing authority should be required to obtain absolute and conclusive proof that this kind of trauma is impossible before granting a license for any procedure which might involve such trauma (paragraph 33).

23. That legislation be implemented the principle aim of which is to safeguard the well-being of the embryo/subject. That such legislation incorporate prohibited procedures in accord with the recommendations made here, that a statutory licensing and regulatory authority be established which is responsible to Parliament and the Secretary of State, and that given the wide range of views and multi-disciplinary concerns raised in the area of embryology that the membership of such an authority be drawn from a wide range of disciplines including philosophy, theology, sociology and medicine. It is recommended that the balance of the authority be weighted against the medical profession and in favour of wider sections of society. The effects of I.V.F. research and correlative programmes may well affect the individual and society in profound ways. The unwanted and unknown effects of such research may be far reaching and unpredictable. We can find no evidence in this area of research

that medicine is so isolated in its potential effects on society that the medical profession would be the best judge in what it might erroneously believe to be its own cause, nor that the medical profession alone is the best determinant of the broader issues which are raised in the areas covered in this document and which, for good or for ill, raise concerns which are far from being merely medical. For good or for ill, the issues raised here may well present problems which affect society as a whole and consequently society as a whole should be skilfully represented in any advisory body or statutory licensing authority.

5

CONCLUSION

At the time of writing, no Bill has been presented to Parliament. It is not therefore possible to comment upon the precise wording of any possible Bill. In most respects concerning the issues surrounding I.V.F. this is unimportant. The Government has made it clear that with the exception of the two optional clauses relating to embryo research, its intentions with regard to the other issues presented are straightforward and will not be the subject of a free vote. Indeed the Government goes so far as to suggest that:

> The proposals set out in this White Paper would constitute one of the most comprehensive and wide ranging pieces of legislation on these issues anywhere in the world... the Government's aim will be to produce legislation which is sufficiently flexible to meet the concerns about these developing reproductive technologies, while recognising the benefits that they can bring.[1]

We recognise that this is a complex task and that the Government is attempting to steer a difficult course between the Scylla of concern and the Charybdis of benefit. Both of these courses are expressed in opposing ethical presuppositions and balancing the putative legitimate claims of opposing factions in this debate is no easy task. We do have some sympathy with the practical and ethical task facing the Government and, to that extent, we are pleased that many recommendations of the kind that we make have been adopted. Three of those recommendations deserve particular mention.

1. The initial wording of the two optional clauses on research into embryos has been substantially altered in the White Paper. We are not entirely satisfied with the re-wording but accept that concerns of the type that we mentioned have been noted.

2. While we did not directly address the issue of surrogacy we did address, by implication, the issue of 'stewardship': an issue examined in greater detail in our opening papers. We note with pleasure that a clear implication of the Government's stance on this issue does imply that the embryo/zygote is not to be regarded as 'property' but as a trust placed in the hands of the community by its agents. While welcoming this development we also found that this stance led to contradictions in the Government's overall position.

3. We also noted that the Government accepts the stance made in our concluding remarks that powers regulating I.V.F. and research into embryos should be vested in a statutory licensing authority responsible to the Secretary of State, and that the Secretary of State should report annually to Parliament. We also noted that the composition of such an authority should be balanced in favour of the laity and against medical members.

These decisions deal with some of our concerns, but they do not deal with the central issue of research into embryos. This is understandable, ostensibly Members of Parliament will be offered a free vote on this issue and to that extent precise wording of the optional clauses will have to wait until the Bill is brought before Parliament. However, as current suggestions stand we must express some reservations.

Cm 46 suggested two optional clauses relating to research on human embryos, which would be presented to Members of Parliament and which would be the subject of a free vote. The first clause would permit certain types of research up to a period of fourteen days after fertilisation, and the second clause would 'prohibit all research except that which was intended to be of benefit to the individual embryo'. It was claimed in Cm 46 that the second clause would have the same objective as the *Unborn Children (Protection) Bills*. The second clause manifestly does not meet that broad objective. The *Unborn Children (Protection) (No. 2) Bill* makes it an offence for any person to

> 'knowingly have in his possession a human embryo produced by *in vitro* fertilisation. Provided that this section shall not apply to an embryo after it has been inserted into a woman.' [2]

The difference between the *Unborn Children (Protection) (No. 2) Bill* and the Government's second optional clause is great. The former implies some notion of strict liability while the latter relies for its force on the notion of intent. In our submission we pointed out some of the dangers inherent in the wording of the optional clauses of Cm 46 and suggested that in the area of embryonic research the distinction between therapeutic research and non-therapeutic research may well be a false one. The addition of the notion of 'intent' merely compounds the elision of this already weak distinction. It is open to any scientist to carry out a wide range of experiments which have no therapeutic benefit to the embryo and to claim that his intention was to enhance the survival of the embryo. There may be cases in which such a claim is correct but there may also be cases in which such a claim merely succeeds in hiding the very research programme that Parliament did not intend to proceed. Cm 259 accepted, in part, this concern expressed in the early part of our submission and in S. 29 pointed out that:

> Those who are opposed to all research involving human embryos argue that procedures which lead to the destruction of the embryo or which make it unsuitable for transfer to a woman should not be permitted in any circumstances. Procedures which do not damage the embryo, or which are actively beneficial to it, do not give the same cause for concern even though such procedures may form part of what some would regard as a programme of research (for example

the observation of embryos developing in different nutrient fluids prior to transfer to a woman).

Our only concern here is that the nutrient fluid should be such that it is known to be not harmful to the embryo. Given the necessity of the use of nutrient fluids we accept that some controlled flexibility in this area is required.

Cm 259 radically alters the wording of Cm 46 with respect to the two optional clauses to be placed before Members of Parliament and takes into account some of the reservations that we expressed in June. The wording for all that leaves much to be desired. S. 30 which covers the issue of research on embyros now offers Members of Parliament two optional clauses expressed as follows:

Prohibiting Research It will be a criminal offence to carry out any procedures on a human embryo other than those aimed at preparing the embryo for transfer to the uterus of a woman; or those carried out to ascertain the suitability of that embryo for the intended transfer.

Permitting Research Except as part of a project specifically licensed by the SLA, it will be a criminal offence to carry out any procedures on a human embryo other than those aimed at preparing the embryo for transfer to the uterus of a woman or those carried out to ascertain the suitability of that embryo for the intended transfer.

On the face of it this formulation appears to restrict research quite markedly regardless of which option is selected. Permitted research appears to be research intended to transfer an embryo to the uterus of a woman. The opening clause, however, makes it clear that far more than this would be permitted. The formulation 'Except as part of a project specifically licensed by the SLA...' makes it clear that except in those cases specifically prohibited by parliament (e.g. research beyond fourteen days, cloning, cross-species fertilisation) any form of research may well be sanctioned by the SLA. Even with the SLA composed of and chaired by the laity, this may turn out to be an insufficient safeguard against procedures and practices not yet themselves well understood or even yet conceptualised.

The first formulation, which appears to restrict research does not entirely overcome our initial objections. The inclusion of the word 'aimed' allows for a considerable degree of latitude on the part of a medical practitioner or scientist and, therefore, a similar kind of objection made against the notion of 'intention' can be levelled at the word 'aimed'. More worrying, the latter part of the formulation of the first clause does allow a medical practitioner or scientist to 'ascertain the suitability of that embryo for the intended transfer.' This formulation could, in itself, hide an experimental programme, indeed its effects might be worse than the second formulation for there is no mention of the SLA in the first formulation. *Hence the clause which intends to prohibit research may well permit research of a broader kind than the clause which intends to allow research.* A second objection which we made, briefly, in the submission still applies to the first clause, and that is that it hides and permits a eugenic programme. We did not deal with this at length in the submission but merely pointed to it and suggested that it would be improper for a hidden eugenic programme tó placed before Parliament without a full and open discussion by Members of Parliament. That objection still applies, and we would extend it further by pointing out that no Government document has actually dealt with, nor invited comments on the eugenic implications of the proposed legislation.

In no sense do we underestimate the difficulties of legislation in the area of embryonic research and in the submission we merely pointed to some guidelines and suggested that the actual task of drafting legislation was sufficiently complex that it should be left to Parliamentary draftsmen. At the same time it should be obvious that we were extremely impressed with the Tate Report in Australia which had the advantage of being able to draw upon the Warnock Committee, the Waller Committee and a wealth of reflective expert evidence. We were also impressed by the submission of St. Vincents Bioethics Centre who suggested in evidence to the Tate Committee that 'prohibited experimenting' means:

> any procedure that involves carrying out research on human embryos of a kind that would be likely to cause damage to the embryo, would be likely to make the embryo unfit for implantation or would be likely to reduce the prospects of a pregnancy resulting from the implantation of the embryo.[3]

This formulation is broadly in line with the suggestion made in our submission that only 'therapeutic intervention which was likely to be of benefit to the individual embryo' should be permitted and that the embryo, as well as the mother, be regarded as a patient (in the moral and clinical sense). Precise drafting, as we have admitted, is difficult, but it is not impossible. It is important that every clause and word of any proposed Bill be subjected to the closest scrutiny. The late Professor Julius Stone summed up the issues in a letter to Senator Brian Harradine where he stated that he was

> '...in general agreement with your position - including the respects in which you go beyond the Waller and Warnock recommendations... this area of research is *par excellence* ' one likely to produce problems for mankind as a whole...'[4]

NOTES

Chapter 1

1. Warnock, M. (Chairman) *Report of the Committee of Inquiry into Human Fertilisation and Embryology.* (London: HMSO Department of Health and Social Security) Cmnd. 9314.
2. Department of Health and Social Security, *Legislation on Human Infertility Services and Embryo Research; A Consultation Paper* (London, HMSO, December 1986) Cm 46.
3. Department of Health and Social Security, *Human Fertilisation and Embryology: A Framework for Legislation* (London: HMSO, November 1987) Cm 259.
4. Ibid., p. 6.
5. Department of Health and Social Security, Cm 46, *op. cit.*, para. 51.
6. Ibid., para. 52.
7. *American Convention on Human Rights, 1969, Article 4.1*, in Sieghart, Paul, *The Lawful Rights of Mankind; An Introduction to the International Legal Code of Human Rights* (Oxford: Oxford University Press, 1986) p. 221.
8. Singer, Peter and Wells, Deane, *The Reproductive Revolution*, (Oxford: OUP, 1984) p. 90.
9. Wiggins, David, *Sameness and Substance* (Oxford: Basil Blackwell, 1980) p. 171.
10. Ibid., pp. 171-172.
11. C v. S, Court of Appeal, Law Report, *The Times*, 25 February 1987.
12. Commonwealth of Australia, Senate Select Committee, Embryo Experimentation Bill, 1985, *Human Embryo Experimentation in Australia* (Canberra: AGPS 1986) Submission No. 256.
13. Warnock, M., op. cit., p. 65.
14. Victoria, Australia, *Infertility (Medical Procedures) Act 1984* (Melbourne: State Government of Victoria, 1984) No. 10163.

15. New Zealand, *Royal Commission of Inquiry into Contraception, Sterilisation and Abortion* p. 184.
16. Pirrie, Michael, 'Fate of Orphaned Embryos hangs on Legal Advice', *The Age*, 7th January 1987.
    'Pressure Grows on Government to Decide Embryo Status', *The Age*, 8 January 1987.

Chapter 2

1. Matthew 25: 40 (all biblical references are to the RSV).
2. Matthew 25: 35-37.
3. Matthew 25: 42-44.
4. See, e.g. Mark 35-45.
5. John 13: 1-20.
6. Luke 4: 18-20.
7. Sheppard, David, *Bias to the Poor* (London: Hodder and Stoughton, 1983) pp. 200 ff.
8. Elliott, Charles, *Praying the Kingdom: Towards a Political Spirituality* (London: Darton, Longman and Todd, 1985) p. 145.
9. Church of England, Board for Social Responsibility, *Human Fertilisation and Embryology;* The Response of the Board for Social Responsibility of the General Synod of the Church of England to the DHSS Report of the Committee of Inquiry. (London: CIO Publishing November 1984) p. 8. This report is a development of its earlier submission to the Warnock Committee: *Evidence to the DHSS (Warnock) Inquiry into Human Fertilisation and Embryology*; Report by the Board for Social Responsibility (London: CIO Publishing, March 1983).
10. Church of England, Board for Social Responsibility, *Personal Origins*; The Report of a Working Party on Human Fertilisation and Embryology of the Board for Social Responsibility (London: CIO Publishing, June 1985) pp. 25-26. This third report is the most developed of the Church of England responses to the question of research on embryos.

11. Ibid., p. 29.
12. The Church of England, Board of Social Responsibility, *Human Fertilisation*.op. cit., p. 8.
13. The Church of England, Board for Social Responsibility, *Personal Origins*, op. cit., p. 28.
14. See e.g. Singer, Peter, *Practical Ethics* (Cambridge: Cambridge University Press, 1979), pp. 131-139.
15. The notion of 'innocency' is one still utilised by Roman Catholic authorities against the use of embryos in research and of course all abortion.
16. Church of England, Board for Social Responsibility, *Personal Origins*, op. cit., p. 31.
17. See e.g. Linzey, Andrew, *Christianity and the Rights of Animals* (London, SPCK, 1987).
18. See e.g. Mark 3: 31-35.
19. Manson, T. W., *The Teaching of Jesus: Studies in its Form and Content* (Cambridge: Cambridge University Press, 1967) p. 306. See also his *Ethics and the Gospel* (London: SCM Press, 1962) esp. pp. 43-57.
20. Matthew 5: 38-42.
21. Manson, T. W., *The Teaching of Jesus* op. cit., p. 299.
22. E.g. Isaiah 1: 17.
23. Clarke, Paul A. B., and Linzey, A., *The Limits to Embryonic Research: A Response to the DHSS Consultation Paper Cm 46*, Centre for the Study of Theology, University of Essex, June 1987, and see below pp. 63-89.
24. Warnock, M., (Chairman), *Report of the Committee*...op.cit.,p. 63, and Church of England, Board for Social Responsibility, *Human Fertilisation*...op.cit., p. 8.
25. Church of England, Board for Social Responsibility, *Personal Origins*, op. cit., p. 15.
26. Ibid., p. 17.
27. Ibid., p. 48.
28. Torrance, T. F., *Divine and Contingent Order*, (Oxford: Oxford University Press, 1981).

29. Church of England, Board for Social Responsibility, *Personal Origins* op. cit., p. 17.
30. Rothschild, Miriam *Animals and Man*, (Oxford: The Clarendon Press, 1986) p. 50.
31. See e.g., the excellent historical survey of Thomas, Keith, *Man and the Natural World: Changing Attitudes in England 1500-1800*, (Harmondsworth: Penguin Books, 1984) esp. pp 100-120.
32. See e.g., Baker, John Austin 'Biblical Attitudes to Nature' in Montefiore, Hugh *Man and Nature* (London: Collins, 1976).
33. *Personal Origins,* op. cit., p. 19.
34. John 16: 13.
35. *Personal Origins,* op. cit., p. 19.
36. Romans 1: 16.
37. Luke 22: 25-27.
38. Trickett, Rachel, 'Imagination and Belief' in Harvey, A. E., (ed.), *God Incarnate: Story and Belief* (London: SPCK, 1981), p. 39; discussed by Horne, B. L., 'Seeing with a Different Eye: Religion and Literature' in Linzey, Andrew, and Wexler, Peter J., (eds.), *Heaven and Earth: Essex Essays in Theology and Ethics* (Worthing, Sussex: Churchman Publishing, 1986) pp. 122-128.
39. Macneice, Louis, 'Prayer Before Birth' in Allott, Kenneth (ed.), *The Penguin Book of Contemporary Verse* (Harmondsworth: Penguin Books, 1966) pp. 194-195.
40. E.g., Matthew 5: 20.
41. See Linzey, Andrew, *Animal Rights: A Christian Assessment* (London: SCM Press, 1975) esp. Chapter 3.

Chapter 3

1. Commonwealth of Australia, *Evidence to the Australian Senate Select Committee on the Human Embryo Experimentation Bill 1985*, (Canberra: AGPS, 1984) pp. 1526-1528.
2. Ibid., pp. 676,724,905,928,1019,1023-1025. In a study at Queen Victoria Medical Centre, Melbourne, Australia, of 314 frozen embryos seven came to term (2.2%).

3. Department of Health and Social Security, Warnock, M. (Chairman), *Report of the Committee*op. cit., p. 66.
4. Commonwealth of Australia, *Evidence*op. cit., 3.5.
5. Ibid., 3.6.
6. Paragraph numbers in parenthesis refer to the paragraphs in the submission and not to paragraph numbers in Cm 46.

Conclusion

1. Department of Health and Social Security, *Human Fertilisation...*op. cit., S. 91.
2. Hargreaves, Ken et. al., *Unborn Children (Protection) (No. 2),* Bill 220, (London: HMSO, October 1986) p. 1.
3. Commonwealth of Australia, Senate Select Committee on Embryo Research...op.cit., p. 52.
4. Ibid., p. 95.

BIBLIOGRAPHY

Bowker, J. W., 'Religions and the Status of the Embryo' in *Human Embryo Research; Yes or No?* (London: Tavistock Publications, 1986), pp. 164-184.

Church of England, Board for Social Responsibility,*Evidence to the DHSS (Warnock) Inquiry into Human Fertilisation and Embryology* (London: CIO Publishing, March 1983).

Human fertilisation and Embryology; The Response of the Board for Social Responsibility of the General Synod of the Church of England to the DHSS Report of the Committee of Inquiry (London: BSR, 1984).

Personal Origins; A Report of a Working Party on Human Fertilisation and Embryology of the Board for Social Responsibility (London: CIO Publishing, March 1985).

The CIBA Foundation, *Human Embryo Research: Yes or No?* (London: Tavistock Publications, 1986).

Commonwealth of Australia, Senate Select Committee on The Human Embryo Experimentation Bill 1985, *Human Embryo Experimentation in Australia* (Canberra: AGPS, September 1986). (Tate Commission).

Ethics in Medical Research; Report of the National Health and Medical Research Council Working Party on Ethics in Medical Research (Canberra: AGPS, 1983).

Department of Health and Social Security, *Human Fertilisation and Embryology: A Framework for Legislation* (London: HMSO, November 1987) Cm 259.

Legislation on Human Infertility Services and Embryo Research; A Consultation Paper (London: HMSO, December 1986) Cm 46.

Warnock, M. (Chairman) *Report of the Committee of Inquiry into Human Fertilisation and Embryology*(London: HMSO, 1984), Cmnd. 9314. (Warnock Report).

Hargreaves, Ken et. al., *Unborn Children (Protection)* (No. 2), Bill 220, (London: HMSO, October 1986).

Jakobovits, Sir Immanuel, *Human Fertilisation and Embryology - A Jewish View; Submissions to the Warnock Committee and The Department of Health and Social Security* (London: Office of the Chief Rabbi, 1984).

Kluvanek, Igor, 'The Argument from Advancement of Science', *St. Vincent's Bioethics Centre Newsletter* September-December 1986, pp. 3-4.

Mahoney, John, *Bioethics and Belief* (London: Sheed and Ward, 1984).

Santamaria, J. N., 'Syngamy and All That', *St. Vincent's Bioethics Centre Newsletter* September, 1987, pp. 1-2.

Singer, Peter, *Practical Ethics* (Cambridge: CUP, 1979).

and Walters, William, *Test-Tube Babies* (Melbourne: OUP, 1982).

Tonti-Filippini, Nicholas, and Daly, T.V., *Experimenting With the Origins of Human Lives; A Submission to the Senate Select Committee on the Human Embryo Experimentation Bill*(Melbourne: St. Vincent's Bioethics Centre, 1985).

Victoria, Australia, State Government, *Infertility (Medical Procedures) Act 1984.* (Waller Committee).